25 Legal Luminaries from 'Vanity Fair'

Lambourn

25 Legal Luminaries from 'Vanity Fair'

by Rupert Collens

Lambourn

London · Dublin · Melbourne

LAMBOURN PUBLICATIONS LTD
12/14 High Road,
London N.2. England
28 Molesworth Street, Dublin 2, Eire
9 Queen Street, Melbourne 3000, Victoria, Australia

First published 1990
©Illustrations - Ruletake Ltd
©Text - Rupert Collens
A limited edition of 500 copies signed and specialy bound in full leather is published
by
The Marlborough Bookshop and Sporting Gallery
6 Kingsbury Street, Marlborough, Wiltshire

Typeset in Garamond and University Roman
DTP Conversion and typesetting by
Typographical Services

ISBN Limited Edition 1-872708-05-6

Trade Edition 1-872708-04-8

Dedication

I dedicate this book with admiration to Clive Burden and his son Philip who have done so much over the last twenty years for all admirers and collectors of *Vanity Fair* in all its aspects, including caricatures. They wear their scholarship lightly and make their knowledge freely available to all of those who enquire. Their shop in Lower Sloane Street, London is a haven for all those interested in *Vanity Fair*.

Author's Thanks

First and foremost, I thank Michael Harris, my researcher, for doing such a magnificent job. I must also thank the staff of The Guildhall Library for their patient help so readily rendered to both Michael and myself. Miles Carpenter, the Manager of Clive A. Burden Ltd., in Sloane Street has been equally helpful. The staff of Holborn Public Library were also most kind.

Next, I must thank Russell March and Vic Prior of March Publications (25 Mount Ephraim, Tunbridge Wells, Kent) for their support and encouragement and their kind permission to plagiarise their original work in *Jockeys of Vanity Fair* and *Cricketers of Vanity Fair*. I do not think I did plagiarise their work but they were kind enough to say I could.

I acknowledge the kind loan of original *Vanity Fair* caricatures from Clive A. Burden Limited, Vic Prior and The Marlborough Bookshop & Sporting Gallery.

I must also thank Jeannine Alexander, the Managing Director of the publishers, for her personal involvement in the project and Peter Fitzmaurice and Philip Hayes of the publishers who have rendered invaluable assistance in checking references.

Key to part
"Bench and Bar"

1. Mr. Gill
2. The Attorney General
3. Lord Coleridge
4. The Solicitor-General
5. Sir Charles Russell Q.C.
6. Mr. R.T. Reid Q.C.
7. Mr. Justice Williams
8. Mr. Cozens-Hardy Q.C.
9. Mr. Jelf Q.C.
10. Mr. Justice Smith
11. Sir Horace Davey Q.C.
12. Baron Pollock
13. Mr. Finlay Q.C.
14. Mr. Graham
15. Mr. Bosanquet Q.C.
16. Mr. Justice Day
17. Mr. Coward
18. Sir Henry James Q.C.

Contents

Pages

6/7 .... Part Group (Bench and Bar) and Key

10/11 .... Introduction

12/13 .... Index/Cross Reference to The 25 Legal Luminaries

15/113 ....The 25 Legal Luminaries

115 ....Table of Case References

117 .... *Nom-de-Crayon* of some Vanity Fair artists

119/123 .... Appendix A - Legal Caricatures by subject

125/126 .... Appendix B - Cross Reference by caption

Introduction

In all probability two factors made *Vanity Fair* the most influential social magazine in the history of the English-speaking world. Firstly, and certainly most obviously, were the weekly caricatures, mainly drawn by SPY. The second factor was the inspiration, ability and drive of its founder and first editor, Thomas Gibson Bowles (1842 - 1922). *Vanity Fair* was the brainchild of Bowles and not surprisingly, as he wrote most of the copy for the first issues of the magazine himself, under pseudonyms such as Blanc Bec, Choker and Auditor. He was the author of the short biographies supporting the caricatures under the name of *Jehu Junior*. This pseudonym was used later by other writers carrying out this function.

The first issue of *Vanity Fair* was published in November 1868, written by Victorians from what is now generally referred to as "the establishment class" and aimed at Victorians of the same standing. Throughout the whole of *Vanity Fair's* life of nearly 50 years, the majority of the circulation was in London and in particular in the "gentlemens' clubs" which proliferated around St. James's.

It was not until the thirteenth issue on 30th January 1869 that the first caricature appeared. This was of Benjamin Disraeli and entitled *He Educated the Tories*. The following week the subject of the caricature was Disraeli's great political rival, William E. Gladstone, which appeared with the caption *Were he a worse man*. It is easy to imagine what a talking point these first two caricatures became in the circles, perhaps best described as "those in the know", which Bowles wished to influence. The finances of the magazine, which had previously been very precarious, took an immediate upturn, and within months of its inception *Vanity Fair* became a highly profitable and very influential publication.

Although the caricatures were the obvious outward sign of *Vanity Fair's* success, the personality of Thomas Gibson Bowles himself was equally important. Tommy was born out of wedlock which, in Victorian days, was normally a severe, if not insurmountable, handicap when trying to enter smart or establishment society. He fully overcame the circumstances of his birth, thanks to his upbringing and his witty and endearing personality. His father, Thomas Milner Gibson, was a man of considerable political and social influence and at one time had been a Member of Parliament and President of the Board of Trade. Although Thomas Milner Gibson and his wife Susanna moved in the most socially correct and conventional circles they were, at the same time, slightly unconventional. Susanna accepted the illegitimate Tommy into the household and brought him up together with the two sons of their marriage. Little or nothing is known of Tommy's natural mother.

Tommy grew up happily in the world of privilege and influence that his father's wealth and position conferred on the family. He was educated in London and spent a few years abroad, but never attended university. For his future career the most important thing was that he had developed a lively and enquiring mind and met a wide variety of people from all walks of life at his stepmother's salon.

Susanna must have been a remarkable woman. Although married to a man who was the epitome of the Victorian establishment, she very much steered her own course through life and ran a lively salon. This, as one would expect, was frequented by the leading lights of the political, literary and artistic world and she was particularly fond of Italians. However, unexpectedly, Susanna was an ardent supporter of early women's rights and involved in spiritualism, the latter being openly practised from time to time in her salon.

The first job which Thomas Gibson Bowles obtained on leaving school was as a junior clerk in the Civil Service at Somerset House, overlooking the Thames. As luck would have it, this could not have been a better situation for the young Bowles. It was close to the Law Courts and, more importantly, Fleet Street, which at that time completely dominated the newspaper and magazine trades. Within a few months of taking up this employment Tommy reached his 20th birthday and found that the work of a junior clerk, with an influential father, was little more than a sinecure. He was fast developing into an extremely handsome and charming man, and was admired by ladies of all ages and classes. Although his father helped him financially, his expenditure in his early years was always to out-run his income, so he was soon "moonlighting" as a part-time journalist.

As well as learning the trade of journalism, Tommy was building up a wide range of friends and acquaintances of the most influential and most promising men of his father's and his own generations, including judges, barristers, solicitors, journalists, actors, politicians and other leaders in society who were soon to appear in *Vanity Fair*.

In mid-1868 Tommy resigned his position as a civil servant and later that year launched *Vanity Fair*, which was started with very limited capital. As already noted, within a few months of starting the magazine it became a great literary and financial success. Bowles was to run it for some 20 years until he sold it to Mr. A. Evans for £20,000 in 1889. In 1892 he followed his father into the House of Commons.

Much of *Vanity Fair's* success and influence can be attributed directly to the caricatures. The first few, including those of Disraeli and Gladstone, were drawn by the Italian, Carlo Pellegrini (1839-1889) whom it is likely that Bowles met at his stepmother's salon and who used the *nom de crayon* "Singe". This was soon anglicised to "Ape" and when the caricatures of Disraeli and Gladstone were reprinted for individual sale, the signature on these was also changed. The early caricatures for *Vanity Fair* made Pellegrini's reputation and he soon became an influential artist, retiring from *Vanity Fair* to work mainly for the Prince of Wales' "Marlborough House Set". Pellegrini's style can be traced via Daumier and the French School back to the English cartoonists of the Georgian era.

Pellegrini was the most influential caricaturist employed by *Vanity Fair*. He set the style and standard which was followed by later artists in particular SPY (Sir Leslie Ward 1851-1922). SPY contributed some 1325 of the 2500 caricatures which appeared in *Vanity Fair*. All the caricatures are often incorrectly referred to as "SPY cartoons". Bowles and his artists always insisted they were caricatures and not cartoons.

The Bench and Bar is universally recognised to have been the genesis of many of the best *Vanity Fair* caricatures. The wigs and robes worn by the subjects acted as props for the artist. The individual caricature was complemented by some of Bowles' most caustic biographies.

Bowles regarded British Law as one of the great institutions of Western Society and was always most careful to praise the ideals and principles of the judicial system, but was by no means overawed by 'The Majesty of the Law'. Bowles was equally willing to draw attention to any deficiency in the legal system and would pick out, sometimes cruelly, any hesitancy or bumbling in manner of the subject.

The first legal caricature appeared on the 11th December, 1869 - *The Lord Justice of England* (Cockburn). This was followed the next week by *A Judge and Peer* (Penzance). From then on the leading Legal Luminaries were to grace *Vanity Fair*. The last caricature to appear was *The Solicitor General* (Buckmaster) on 19th November, 1913. Only ten more caricatures appeared before *Vanity Fair* vanished into *Hearth and Home*.

The caricatures of judges, barristers, solicitors and other members of the legal profession have long been avidly collected, not only by the legal profession itself, but by many others throughout the world. The "Red Judges", until the recent rise in demand for sportsmen, especially cricketers, golfers and polo players, used to command a considerable premium over most other *Vanity Fair* caricatures.

Over the years the layout of the caricatures in *Vanity Fair* changed, as did the type of paper on which they were printed. The most noticeable change was that up until 1873 the prints were framed by black lines, crossing at the corners.

Without wishing to be pedantic as there were many exceptions to the rule, from 1869 to 1874, the colour printing was done by *Rankin & Cox*. From 1874 until late 1911 the printing was done by *Vincent Brooks, Day & Son* who were responsible for the best quality of printing in *Vanity Fair*. Normally their imprint appeared just below and to the left-hand corner of the caricature. When they took over from *Rankin & Cox*, the quality of the paper used improved, which greatly enhanced the colour reproduction.

In 1911 *Vincent Brooks, Day & Son's* factory burnt down and for the next two years many different printers were used, before printing returned to their rebuilt factory in 1913.

The caricatures were normally reproduced in three versions: Firstly they appeared in the weekly magazine itself, with the biography opposite as part of the normal letterpress set in column width. The more successful caricatures were reprinted for individual re-sale with a re-set and sometimes slightly edited biography. The third method was the half-yearly or yearly *Vanity Fair Albums* which were beautifully bound in green cloth, with the top and side edges gilt.

The magazine changed slowly but steadily after Bowles sold it in 1889 and by the mid-1890's had become very "gossipy" and little more than a record of Society's doings. Even before the outbreak of the First World War, the magazine, which for so long had been one of the greatest publications of its type, had failed and in February 1914 it was absorbed by *Hearth and Home*.

The 25 Legal Luminaries

By Title (where appropriate)

BIRKENHEAD, Earl see .... FREDERICK EDWIN SMITH

BRAMPTON, Baron see .... HENRY HAWKINS

CARSON OF DUNCAIRN, Baron see .... EDWARD HENRY CARSON

COZENS-HARDY, Baron see .... HERBERT HARDY COZENS-HARDY

DARLING, Baron see .... CHARLES JOHN DARLING

FARNBOROUGH, Baron see .... THOMAS ERSKINE MAY

GORDON OF DRUMEARN, Baron see .... EDWARD STRATHEARN GORDON

READING, Marquis see .... RUFUS DANIEL ISAACS

RUSSELL OF KILLOWEN, Lord see .... CHARLES RUSSELL

TREVETHIN, Baron see .... ALFRED TRISTRAM LAWRENCE

FAMILY NAMES

McNEILL, DUNCAN .... LORD COLONSAY AND ORONSAY

SHAND, ALEXANDER BURNS .... BARON SHAND

The 25 Legal Luminaries

SUBJECT	CAPTION	PAGE
THOMAS BEARD	"UNDER SHERIFF"	15
GAINSFORD BRUCE	"SLOW AND STEADY"	19
EDWARD HENRY CARSON	"I NEVER ASK ANYONE TO DO ANYTHING"	23
JOSEPH WILLIAM CHITTY	"THE UMPIRE"	27
ALEXANDER JAMES EDMUND COCKBURN	"THE LORD CHIEF JUSTICE OF ENGLAND"	31
LORD COLONSAY AND ORONSAY	"SCOTCH LAW"	35
HERBERT HARDY COZENS-HARDY	"FAIR, IF NOT BEAUTIFUL"	39
CHARLES JOHN DARLING	"JUDICIAL LIGHTWEIGHT"	43
HENRY FIELDING DICKENS	"HIS FATHER INVENTED PICKWICK"	47
EDWARD STRATHEARN GORDON	"LORD ADVOCATE"	51
HENRY HAWKINS	"THE TICHBORNE CASE"	55
RUFUS DANIEL ISAACS	"RUFUS"	59
GEORGE JESSEL	"THE LAW"	63
FITZ ROY KELLY	"THE LORD CHIEF BARON"	67
ROBERT MALCOLM KERR	"THE CITY OF LONDON COURT"	71
ALFRED TRISTRAM LAWRENCE	"LORRY"	75
GEORGE HENRY LEWIS	"AN ASTUTE LAWYER"	79
CHARLES WILLIE MATHEWS	"HE CAN MARSHAL EVIDENCE"	83
THOMAS ERSKINE MAY	"PARLIAMENTARY PRACTICE"	87
CHARLES EDWARD POLLOCK	"ONE OF THE FAMILY"	91
CHARLES RUSSELL	"A SPLENDID ADVOCATE"	95
THOMAS EDWARD SCRUTTON	"COPYRIGHT"	99
BARON SHAND	"A SCOTS LAWYER"	103
ARCHIBALD LEVIN SMITH	"3RD COMMISSIONER"	107
FREDERICK EDWIN SMITH	"NO SURRENDER"	111

THOMAS BEARD

Parentage:
Born: 28th April 1828 in Devonshire.

Career:
Professional:
1838 - Practised as a solicitor at 10 Basinghall Street where he continued to his death.
1869 - Member of the Common Council of the City of London for Bassishaw Ward until his death.
1872 - 1874 - Undersheriff of the City of London.
1886 - 1890 - Deputy for Bassishaw Ward.
1887 - 1888 - Undersheriff of the City of London. Master of the Fruiterers Company and Master of the Loriners Company.
1889 - 1891 - Undersheriff of the City of London.
1892 - 1894 - Undersheriff of the City of London.

General:
A leading Freemason and a member of several lodges.

Died:
10th June 1895 at Putney.

Little is known of the early life of Thomas Beard except that he hailed from Devon. He was articled as a solicitor in the City of London and in due course set up his own practice at 10 Basinghall Street. He was for 37 years a member of Common Council for this ward and served for four years as deputy.

He frequently served as Undersheriff whose duties included execution of writs, the empanelling of juries at The Old Bailey, the Mayor's Court and the City of London Court.

A grimmer task was to supervise the execution of prisoners in Newgate; public executions had ceased there in 1868. From 1877 until 1902, its date of demolition, Newgate was used solely as a place of confinement for prisoners sentenced to death at The Old Bailey. The quaint old custom of tolling the bell of St. Sepulchre's Church opposite the prison for quarter-of-an-hour before the executions was continued to the end.

Thomas Beard was a popular and social man, a Master of two Livery Companies and a leading Freemason.

MR. THOMAS BEARD

HE was born three-and-sixty years ago, and while still quite young he came to London to learn, in a solicitor's office, the significance of pink tape and the intricacies of the criminal law, until such time as he might practice on his own account. Since then he has defended, or has prepared the defence of, many wicked men: some of them so wicked that he could not save them; as were Franz Muller, who was hanged for the murder of Mr. Briggs in a railway carriage, and the mutineers of the *Lennie*. For more than twenty years he has been attached to the Corporation of London, being well known as a Chairman of Committees; and he is now serving as Under-Sheriff for the sixth time.

He is fond of the Play, and he is quite a popular man in the City, being looked upon as a good fellow. He has so much respect for the Law that he has put two sons into it; so that he now has most of his professional work done for him.

"Under Sheriff"

GAINSFORD BRUCE

"SLOW AND STEADY"   **6th December 1900**

Parentage:
Born: 1834, eldest son of John Collingwood Bruce and Charlotte, daughter of Tobias Gainsford of Gerrards Cross, Bucks.

Educated:
Glasgow University.

Career:
Professional:
1859 - Called to the Bar.
1877 - Recorder of Bradford.
1879 - Solicitor-General of the County Palatine of Durham.
1883 - Queen's Counsel.
1886 - Attorney-General of the County Palatine of Durham.
1887 - Chancellor of the County Palatine of Durham.
1892 - Appointed a Judge of the Queen's Bench Division of the High Court of Justice and Knighted.
1904 - Retired and sworn of the Privy Council.

Political:
1888 - Elected M.P. for the Holborn Division of Finsbury. Re-elected 1892 resigning on his elevation to the Bench.

General:
A keen yachtsman. Member of the Royal Yacht Squadron, Cowes.

Personal:
1868 - Married Sophia, daughter of Francis Jackson.

Died:
24th February 1912.

Gainsford Bruce came of a Scottish family, although born and brought up in Buckinghamshire. He finished his education at Glasgow University. After he was called to the Bar he practised on the Northern Circuit. He specialised in Admiralty.

However he exhibited considerable professional versatility for a civilian by becoming Chancellor of the County Palatine of Durham, a Court of Equity, and a Judge of the Queen's Bench Division, a Common Law Court.

His interest in matters maritime was not confined to legal aspects for as well as being the editor of *Maude & Pollock on Shipping* and co-author of *Williams & Bruce on Admiralty Practice,* he enjoyed yachting and was made a member of the Royal Yacht Squadron.

The caricature has caught the subject brilliantly as although he was recognised as a good judge in both commercial and civil cases, he was also painfully slow. His "medicine" was known to be of the alcoholic type.

MR. JUSTICE GAINSFORD BRUCE

THIS Judge of eight years' standing and six-and-sixty years of age is a Glasgow University man and a Durham Doctor of Civil Law, who began his career at the Bar forty years ago. He held various offices quite adequately, he helped to write a book on Admiralty Practice and another on Shipping, he was in Parliament for a time (after four repulses), and now, though the slowest, is far from being the least unworthy occupant of Her Majesty's Bench. He has attended the four annual Assizes at Manchester and Liverpool, and is supposed to have given more satisfaction to the merchants of those northern towns than have many of his more brilliant and versatile brethren. He is a very careful, conscientious, hard-working Judge, who takes a long time to master the evidence and the law of a case; but having mastered them, he very seldom goes wrong in his judgment. He is also a severe Churchman, who has been nominated to exercise the jurisdiction of a Judge under the Benefices' Act of 1898; yet he has been known to laugh. In the Admiralty Court he was once obliged to read an entry in the ship's log according to which the crew had found it "very slow work pushing the old Bruce along."

Altogether he is quite a good Judge, and those who know him affirm that he is not so depressing a companion as his cast of visage would seem to imply.

"slow and steady."

EDWARD HENRY CARSON
(Baron Carson of Duncairn)

"I NEVER ASK ANYONE TO DO ANYTHING"   **17th January 1912**

Parentage:
Born: 9th February 1854 in Dublin, second son of Edward Henry Carson, a civil engineer practising in that city and Isabella, daughter of Captain Peter Lambert of Castle Ellen, Athenry, Co. Galway, a descendant of General John Lambert.

Educated:
Portarlington School and Trinity College, Dublin.

Career:
Professional:
1877 - Called to the Bar of King's Inns, Dublin.
1887 - Junior Counsel to the Attorney-General.
1889 - Queen's Counsel in Ireland.
1891 - Bencher of King's Inns, Dublin.
June 1892 - Solicitor-General for Ireland.
1893 - Called to the Bar of the Middle Temple.
1894 - Queen's Counsel in England.
1896 - Sworn of the Irish Privy Council
1900 - Solicitor-General for England. Knighted. Elected Bencher of the Middle Temple.
December 1905 - Went out of office. Sworn of the Privy Council in England.
May 1915 - Attorney-General.
October 1916 - Resigned office.
1921 - Appointed Lord of Appeal in Ordinary as Baron Carson of Duncairn.
1922 - Treasurer of the Middle Temple.

Political:
July 1892 - Elected as one of the M.P.'s for Dublin University and held the seat for 26 years.
January 1910 - Chosen as Leader of the Unionists.
December 1916 - First Lord of the Admiralty.
July 1917 - Left the Admiralty to become a member of the War Cabinet.
January 1918 - Resigned from the Government over Lloyd George's Home Rule Bill.
December 1918 - Elected M.P. for the newly created constituency of the Duncairn Division of Belfast.
1921 - Resigned as Leader of the Unionists.

Personal:
1872 - Married (1) Sarah Annette Foster (d.1913), adopted daughter of Henry Perse Kirwan of Triston Lodge, Co. Galway. Had issue two sons and two daughters of whom the elder son and younger daughter predeceased him. (2) In 1914, Ruby, elder daughter of Lieutenant Colonel Stephen Frewen (afterwards Frewen-Laton) of Winton and Sigston Castle, Yorks. Had issue one son.

Died:
22nd October 1935 at Cleve Court, Minster, Kent. He was given a State Funeral in Belfast and buried in St. Anne's Cathedral.

Edward Carson was born and educated in Dublin, being called to the Irish Bar in 1877. He practised in Dublin and on the Leinster Circuit with considerable success and made the transition to the London Bar painlessly.

He entered Parliament in 1892 and although one of the foremost advocates of his day, it is as the champion of the Unionist cause at Westminster he is best remembered. In 1911 he was invited by the Ulster Unionist Council to frame a constitution for the provisional government of that province and in 1912 he raised the Ulster Volunteer Force. Permission to drill was readily granted by the Magistrates and soon battalions were raised all over the province. In January 1913 he personally contributed £10,000 to its funds.

In April 1914, when gun-running into Larne by the Ulster Volunteer Force was denounced by Asquith in the House of Commons, Carson rose and accepted full responsibility for everything that had been done.

Carson was one of the few men to be appointed a Lord of Appeal in Ordinary without having held any judicial office but he took an active part in the judicial business of the House.

RT. HON. SIR EDWARD HENRY CARSON, KT., P.C., M.P., K.C., LL.D.

When Providence created Sir Edward Carson there was a rattle among the cobblestones at the Old Bailey. The story is that after his eloquence had spent itself, and a good deal of Treasury money, for a year of two, the old place became nervous and had to be rebuilt. Evildoers trembled as they watched the face of Carson; it was a face meant for them.

Yet this eminent man always leaves the Court without a stain upon his character.

He is really, by profession, a homoeopathic medicine. He convicted moonlighters in 1887 as he hopes to convict limelighters in 1912 by means of an Irish brogue. He defeats Irish ideas by means of his Irish pronunciation. He is the only surviving man who has called Mr. Lewis Harcourt a "sneak." But he is in line to get there, just the same.

His voice is as soft as swansdown. He is as gentle in his speech as if he were a Welshman. But he may use a megaphone when he leads the Army of Ulster - the megaphone being supplied by F.E. Smith and Co.

The chief things he has tried for were to clear young Archer-Shee and get damages for Lever's against the "Daily Mail." No man ever fought harder in either case, and poor Rufus had to sit up all night, with wet towels, trying to escape the toils. If Sir Edward Carson can do such things off his own bat, what will he not accomplish with Captain Craig to help him?

Would that his health were stronger. No man can serve two masters, and Sir Edward has fallen between Law and Politics, with a dash of Protestantism added - hard on the digestion.

He has no enemies - is most popular at Pentonville - and will exercise a Mollie-Maguiring effect on College Green, if it ever comes to that.

In the meantime, he may be discovered any midnight practising in a rifle club - basement - whence the dearth in picture-postcards of Mr. Winston Churchill.

He likes an Orange.

"I never ask anyone to do anything
which I will not do myself."

JOSEPH WILLIAM CHITTY

"THE UMPIRE"   **28th March 1885**

Parentage:
Born: 1828 in Calthorpe Street, Gray's Inn Road, second son of Thomas Chitty, the celebrated special pleader, admitted in 1820 at the age of 19 and who continued to attend his chambers at 1 King's Bench Walk for 57 years. He was the grandson of the yet more famous Joseph Chitty, the author of a series of 20 standard practitioner's text books.

Educated:
Eton and Baliol College, Oxford. In 1851 graduated B.A. (First in Greats): 1852 Elected Vinerian scholar and fellow of Exeter College. 1855 - Proceeded M.A.

Career:
Professional:
1851 - Entered Lincoln's Inn.
1856 - Called to the Bar of Lincoln's Inn.
1874 - Queen's Counsel.
1875 - Elected Bencher of Lincoln's Inn.
1881 - Appointed Judge of the High Court of Justice, Chancery Division.
1882 - Knighted.
1895 - Treasurer of Lincoln's Inn.
1897 - Appointed Lord Justice of Appeal.
1898 - Nominated Judge under the Benefice Act of that year. Died in office.

Political:
April 1880 - Elected M.P. for Oxford in the Liberal interest in the General Election and held the seat until his elevation to the Bench.

General:
1850, 1851, 1852 - Stroked the Oxford boat to victory. Twice kept the Oxford wicket.
1857 - 1881 - Umpire of Inter-University Boat Race.
1867 - 1877 - Major, Inns of Court Volunteer Corps.

Personal:
1858 - Married Clara Jessie, daughter of the Rt. Hon. Sir Frederick Pollock, C.B.

Died:
15th February 1899 at 33 Queen's Gate Gardens, Hyde Park and buried in Brookwood Cemetery.

Joseph Chitty was the son and grandson of distinguished lawyers and legal writers and himself was one of the most distinguished judges of the 19th Century. His father, Thomas, edited *Archbold,* the criminal bible, *Burn's Justice of the Peace* and wrote *Chitty's Forms.* He was educated at Eton and Baliol College, Oxford, was a great oarsman, both at school and University, stroking the Oxford team to three consecutive victories in 1850, 1851 and 1852.

He was an eminent Chancery lawyer who, on the Bench, decided many important cases under the Settled Land Act of 1882. Appeals from his judgments were rare, and even more rarely successful.

He enjoyed a reputation as a wit, two of his most famous remarks being: "Truth will sometimes leak out, even through an Affidavit" and *"Fiat justitia, ruat coelum"* when the ceiling of his courtroom collapsed.

THE HON. SIR JOSEPH WILLIAM CHITTY

EVER since these isles were peopled, some Chitty or other has been always writing or editing books about English Law. The present Judge of this distinguished name is not the offspring of Chitty's Statutes or of Chitty on Contracts, but of Chitty's Archbold - that is to say, he is the second son of the late Mr. Thomas Chitty, who was a very eminent and popular Special Pleader in his day.

Born seven-and-fifty years ago, young Joseph William was sent to Eton to do sums and learn his Latin grammar; and then, having proceeded to Balliol College, Oxford, by the aid of diligence and good ability he took a First Class in Classics in 1851, afterwards being elected a Fellow of Exeter, and becoming Vinerian Scholar in 1852. Of course he next went in for Law; in 1856 was called to the Bar at Lincoln's Inn (of which he was made a Bencher nineteen years later), took silk in 1874, grew to be the Leader in the Rolls Court, and carried on an enormous practice. Strange to say, he omitted to pose as a legal author. Presently he drifted into politics, and in 1880 he sat as a Liberal M.P. for corrupt Oxford, in which posture he might possibly have remained, had he not, in September, 1881, been appointed a Judge of the Chancery Division in the room of Sir George Jessel, who was moved on to the Court of Appeal.

Like his father, Sir Joseph has always been a favourite with his fellow-men; and, being of a robust frame, he from time to time distinguished himself in various athletic exercises. He rowed for his University, he took much interest in the Inns of Court Volunteers (of which he was a Major), and for many years he officiated as the Umpire at the Oxford and Cambridge Boat-Race. When raised to the dignity of the Bench, however, he put away umpiring and lawn-tennis and similar childish things. In Court he is agreeable, although his voice is very penetrating; but business progresses rather slowly there - they say because he wants to talk quite as much as the Counsel appearing before him; wherefore they irreverently call him "Mr. Justice Chatty."

"The Umpire"

ALEXANDER JAMES EDMUND COCKBURN

"THE LORD CHIEF JUSTICE OF ENGLAND"   **11th December 1869**

Parentage:

Born: 24th December 1802, the only son of Alexander Cockburn, British envoy extraordinary and Minister Plenipotentiary to the State of Colombia and of Yolande, daughter of the Viscomte de Vignier. His father was of an ancient Scottish family. His uncles included Sir James, 7th Bart. (1771-1852), who was Major-General, Under-Secretary for War and for the Colonies (1806-1807) and Governor of the Bermudas (1811), Sir George, 8th Bart. (1772 - 1853), who was an Admiral and Sir William (1773-1858) 9th Bart., who was Dean of York.

Educated:

Privately, both at home and on the continent and Trinity Hall, Cambridge. In 1829 he took the degree of B.C.L. with First Class Honours and was elected a fellow.

Career:

Professional:

1825 - Entered the Middle Temple.

1829 - Called to the Bar and joined the Western Circuit.

1832 - Published a volume of reports of election cases in collaboration with Mr. Rowe.

1841 - Recorder of Southampton and Queen's Counsel.

July 1850 - Solicitor-General and Knighted.

1850 - February 1852 - Attorney-General.

December 1852 - November 1856 - Attorney-General.

1853 - Treasurer of the Middle Temple.

1854 - Recorder of Bristol.

November 1856 - Lord Chief Justice of the Common Pleas.

June 1859 - Lord Chief Justice of England. Declined a peerage. Died in office.

1872 - Arbitrator for the British Government at the "Alabama" arbitration under the Treaty of Washington held at Geneva. Again refused a peerage but accepted G.C.B.

Political:

1847 - Elected unopposed at Southampton in the Liberal interest and held the seat until elevated to the Bench.

Personal:

A bachelor.

Died:

20th November 1890 suddenly at 40 Hertford Street, Mayfair. Buried in the family vault at Kensal Green.

Alexander Cockburn was half French, which probably accounted for his being such a good linguist. He spoke fluent French, German, Spanish and Italian and naturally had a good command of Latin and Ancient Greek. He was a great scholar winning prizes at Cambridge for English and Latin and was a candidate for the Mastership of Trinity Hall in 1852 and again in 1877.

Cockburn made his name by reports on election cases which quickly established him as a leading lawyer in these matters, then of considerable importance owing to the passage of the Reform Bill in 1832. He was appointed a Member of the Commission of Enquiry into the state of Corporations in England and Wales in 1834.

He was Leading Counsel for Daniel McNaughten [(1843) 10 Cl. Fin 200] who shot Mr. Drummond, Sir Robert Peel's Secretary, in mistake for the Prime Minister himself. Cockburn obtained McNaughten's acquital on the grounds of his insanity and it was the Opinion of the Judges, delivered to the House of Lords following this case, which laid down the celebrated McNaughten Rules which still govern the subject. He led for the prosecution in the case of William Palmer, "The Rugby Poisoner" and obtained his conviction.

Cockburn presided in what was, perhaps, the trial of the century, "The Tichborne Case" which lasted 188 days, Cockburn's summing up lasting 18 of these [R. v. Orton or Castro (1874) L.R. 9 QB, 350]. In 1872 he represented the British Government in the "Alabama" arbitration at Geneva under the Treaty of Washington.

THE RIGHT HONOURABLE
SIR ALEXANDER J.E. COCKBURN, BART.

THE Judges are perhaps the only public functionaries in England who command and obtain universal respect. It is the redeeming feature of our system of government that, amid universal distrust and discredit, the administration of justice has been kept pure, and that its conduct is committed to men whose ability and impartiality are above all suspicion. The Lord Chief Justice is, as becomes him, the most laborious of all the Judges: he never tires or falters, but patiently follows all things and endures all things, so that he is held to be the only Judge who really tries a case upon its full merits.

Endowed by nature with the private and personal qualities that win affection from most men and all women, Sir Alexander would have made himself eminent in any sphere of life. His public career has been also favoured by political opportunities. Liberal even to Radicalism in his opinions, he first distinguished himself in Parliament by an admirable piece of advocacy in the Pacifico debate. This speech was enviously called a specimen of the "Freemasons' Tavern school of oratory," but it was perfectly adapted to the occasion, and Lord Palmerston, as was his wont, never afterwards lost an opportunity of showing his gratitude for the good service he had then received. But the Lord Chief Justice cannot receive any increase of honour or respect. Having become a baronet in spite of himself, he refused to be made a peer, and thereby escapes the risk that peers run of transmitting his honours to descendants who might have no other claim to them than the mere accident of birth.

"The Lord Chief Justice of England"

LORD COLONSAY AND ORONSAY
(Duncan McNeill)

"SCOTCH LAW"   **13th September 1873**

Parentage:

Born: August 1793 in the island of Oronsay, Argyllshire, second but eldest surviving son of John McNeill of Colonsay and Oronsay, a notable agriculturalist and improver of the breed of highland cattle, and of Hester, eldest daughter of Duncan McNeill of Dunmore, Argyllshire. He was brother of Sir John McNeill, the diplomat.

Educated:

University of St. Andrews, taking Honours in Mathematics and graduating M.D. University of Edinburgh, reading law.

Career:

Professional:

1816 - Called to the Scottish Bar.

1820 - Advocate-Depute.

1824 - Sheriff of Perthshire.

November 1834 - April 1835 - Solicitor-General for Scotland.

September 1841 - October 1842 - Solicitor-General for Scotland.

October 1842 - July 1846 - Lord Advocate.

1843 - Dean of Faculty. He continued to be re-elected annually until raised to the Bench.

1851 - Appointed Ordinary Lord of Session and assumed the style and title of Lord Colonsay and Oronsay.

1852 - Appointed Lord Justice-General and Lord President of the Court of Session and sworn of the Privy Council.

1867 - Created Baron Colonsay and Oronsay on his retirement. He took his share in the judicial business of the House, the first Scottish lawyer raised to the peerage for that purpose.

Political:

1843 - 1851 - M.P. for Argyllshire.

Personal:

A bachelor.

Died:

31st January 1874 at Pau in France.

Duncan McNeill, who was created Lord Colonsay and Oronsay in 1867, having taken the title as a Judge in the Court of Session in 1851, came from prosperous farming folk in Argyllshire. His father was one of the leading stock breeders in Scotland and his father's portrait hangs in the National Portrait Gallery in Edinburgh.

Duncan McNeill was called to the Scottish Bar where he practiced mainly Criminal Law. In 1842 he became Lord Advocate which was in effect the Secretary of State for Scotland and in that capacity McNeill introduced the Scottish Poor Law Bill.

He rose to be Lord Justice-General, the head of the High Court of Justiciary, the highest criminal court in Scotland, and Lord President head of the Court of Session, the highest civil court; these two offices always being held by the same individual.

He was the first Scottish lawyer to be raised to the peerage for the purpose of hearing Scottish appeals.

LORD COLONSAY

FOR a young Scotchman who has set his hopes across the Border there is no more promising profession than the Law, and there is none in which Scotchmen have gained so disproportionate a share of prizes. Wherefore presumably it was that John McNeill sent his boy Duncan to the working University of St. Andrew's, and then to the Scottish Bar. This was nigh upon sixty years ago and Duncan, now a hale old gentleman of over eighty, has passed since then through every kind of official post until he arrived at last safely in the haven of the House of Lords. He has been successively Sheriff of Perthshire, Solicitor-General for Scotland, Lord Advocate, Dean of the Faculty of Advocates, a Lord of Session, and finally Lord Justice-General and President of the Court of Session, until upon his retirement he was permanently installed upon the red benches. He is one of the old Conservatives who believed in Peel, and he still continues a member of the Carlton while many of his former friends have crossed to the Reform. He fitly represents the Majesty of Scotch Law, invested with the Mercy of a British Peerage.

"Scotch Law"

HERBERT HARDY COZENS-HARDY
(Baron Cozens-Hardy)

"FAIR, IF NOT BEAUTIFUL"   **24th January 1901**

Parentage:
Born: 22nd November 1838 at Letheringsett Hall, Dereham, Norfolk, second son of William Hardy Cozens-Hardy, solicitor in Norwich and Sarah, daughter of Thomas Theobald.

Educated:
Amersham Hall School and University College, London. Graduated 1858. LL.B. 1863 Member of Senate and fellow of University College, London. 1871-1876 Examiner in Equity and Real Property.

Career:
Professional:
1862 - Called to the Bar of Lincoln's Inn after obtaining a Studentship and Certificate of Honour.
1882 - Queen's Counsel.
1899 - Appointed a Judge of the High Court, Chancery Division and Knighted.
1901 - Lord Justice of Appeal and sworn of the Privy Council.
March 1907 - Master of the Rolls.
1913 - One of the three Commissioners of the Great Seal during the absence of Haldane, L.C., in Canada.
1914 - Raised to the peerage as 1st Baron Cozens-Hardy of Letheringsett.
1918 - Retired.
Also
Chairman of the Council for Legal Education, a Chairman of Norfolk Quarter Sessions, Bencher of Lincoln's Inn, Chairman General Council of the Bar.

Political:
1885 - 1899 - M.P. for North Norfolk in the Liberal interest at the General Election and continued to sit for that constituency until elevated to the Bench.

Personal:
1866 - Married Maria (d.1886) daughter of Thomas Hepburn of Clapham Common. Two sons and two daughters.

Died:
18th June 1920 at Letheringsett Hall. Buried at Kensal Green.

Hardy Cozens-Hardy came from an East Anglian Congregationalist family at a time in the middle of the 19th Century when Congregationalists were particularly influential in the Liberal Party. Like many dissenters of the period, he studied at the University of London.

Soon after being called to the Bar he built up an excellent Chancery practice, both at first instance and on appeal. His non-conformist connections brought him much business. For that reason he did not apply for silk for some 20 years.

Ever since the appointment of Jessell, M.R. (q.v.), the activities of the Master of the Rolls were confined to the Court of Appeal of which he was President. In fulfilling this role, Cozens-Hardy did not merely deal with equity matters with distinction, but showed a hitherto unexpected mastery of the Common Law.

Probably his best remembered case at the Bar was that of Bradford Corporation v. Pickles [(1895) - AC.587] in which a farmer threatened that unless the Corporation purchased his land he would drill bore-holes to prevent water from the land reaching the Corporation's reservoirs. An Injunction was refused on the grounds that malice did not render an otherwise lawful act unlawful.

THE HON. MR. JUSTICE COZENS-HARDY

IT has been said already that by birth, by social position, and by education he is a Radical; for one-and-sixty years ago he became the son of Mr. William Cozens-Hardy, of Letheringsett, in Norfolk: who was a Liberal Justice of the Peace; and a few years later he began his education at Amersham, to continue it at University College, London, and at the feet of Mr. Gladstone. He is a Fellow of University College, a double graduate of London University, a member of the Reform Club, and a very excellent, absolutely honest Judge. He began to practise at the Bar forty years ago; and he took to Equity and Real Property Law so kindly that nine years later he was chosen to examine in those dry subjects on behalf of London University. Twenty years of quiet, painstaking practice brought him to silk, when he had long been known in Lincoln's Inn as one of the best of all the Juniors in Chancery. Then he became the only leader in Mr. Justice North's Court. At the Bar he was known for his integrity; being so very honest and so openly candid that the most suspicious Judge was never unready to put his trust in him; and withal he was a careful, precise, and hardworking student of Law. Although he knows something about patents, he was, as a Member of Parliament, able to swallow Home Rule; but now he has been a ornament of the Bench for nearly two years. Since Lord Justice Romer made room for him there, none finds fault in him.

He is not a vain man; yet is he as fair a Judge as he is uncomely.

"fair, if not beautiful"

CHARLES JOHN DARLING
(Baron Darling)

"JUDICIAL LIGHT WEIGHT"   **8th May 1907**

Parentage:
Born: 6th December 1849 at Abbey House, Colchester, Essex, elder son of Charles Darling, afterwards of Langham Hall, Essex, a member of a Border family who managed estates and farmed on his own account in the neighbourhood, and of Sarah Frances, daughter of John Tizard of Dorchester.

Educated:
Privately.

Career:
Professional:
1872 - Having been for a short time articled to a firm of Birmingham solicitors entered Inner Temple.
1874 - Called to the Bar of the Inner Temple.
1885 - Queen's Counsel.
1892 - Elected a Bencher of the Inner Temple.
1896 - Commissioner of Assize on the Oxford Circuit.
October 1897 - Appointed a Judge of the Queen's Bench Division of the High Court of Justice.
1917 - Sworn of the Privy Council, having, as senior puisne, served as Lord Reading's deputy during his absence in the U.S.A.
November 1923 - Retired.
January 1924 - Created Baron Darling of Langham. Served as a member of the Judicial Committee of the Privy Council and as late as 1931 returned to the King's Bench Division to assist in reducing arrears of work.

Political:
December 1885 - Contested South Hackney as a Conservative.
July 1886 - Again contested the seat against Sir Charles Russell, afterwards Lord Russell of Killowen (q.v.).
February 1888 - Returned as M.P. for Deptford in a by-election and held the seat until elevated to the Bench.

General:
1912 - Member of the Royal Commission on the working of the King's Bench.
1919 - Chairman of the Committee on Court Martial.
1925 - Chairman of the Committee on the Moneylenders Bill.
1928 - Chairman of the Committee on national marks.

Personal:
1885 - Married Mary Caroline (d.1913), elder daughter of Major-General William Wilberforce Harris Greathed, R.E. veteran of the Indian Mutiny and granddaughter of Caroline Clive. One son who predeceased him and two daughters.

Died:
29th May 1936 at Lymington. Succeeded as 2nd Baron by his grandson Robert Charles Henry (b.1919).

Charles Darling was educated privately and was for a time articled to a firm of Birmingham solicitors, before reading for the Bar. He enjoyed the patronage of a very rich lady whom he called "aunt" and who left him a most comfortable fortune.

He joined the Oxford Circuit to which his practice was wholly confined, where he failed to distinguish himself. His appointment as Commissioner of Assize was made a political issue by the Liberals who claimed that it was "an office of profit under the Crown" and that in accepting it he had vacated his seat in the House of Commons. Darling pointed out that he had refused any payment.

He elevation to the Bench was thought to be political and the editor of one Birmingham newspaper was fined for contempt for describing him as "a microcosm of pomposity in ermine" and regretted that "the Lord Chancellor had no other relative to provide for amongst the larrikins of the law on the day he appointed Mr. Justice Darling". Concerning his "aunt", the paper said that "that misguided testator *(sic)* spoiled an excellent bus conductor".

He was noted for his witticisms from the Bench and on one occasion when he asked Counsel "who is Mr. George Robey?", Counsel replied aptly "he is the Darling of the music halls". He was an able and learned judge and presided in the Casement appeal [(1917) 1 K.B. 98].

THE HON. MR. JUSTICE DARLING

CERTAIN people are born great; others have greatness thrust upon them. Mr. Justice Darling is one of the others. We have been in his Court on various and sundry occasions. He has reclined in his chair in pretty much the manner of any other King's Bench Judge, and the proceedings have been dull and wearisome. Occasionally my Lord would say a word - quite a simple, commonplace word. And for some reasons beyond the ken of an ordinary person, the Court straightway rippled with laughter.

I shall not venture on the assertion that the Hon. Mr. Justice Darling is not a wit. At least two of his published works tend to prove that he does possess the divinest of faculties, but it is a faculty which, in my Lord's case, appears to express itself at the end of a pen rather than at the tip of a tongue.

On the other hand, the newspaper reporters of this world, not to mention the Junior Bar, are convinced that Mr. Justice Darling is a sort of Mr. Plowden among judges, and consequently when he opens his mouth from the bench we giggle as one man. And Mr. Justice Darling reaps the benefit in head lines of the "witty Judge" order, and the respect of the Junior Bar.

Cutting the cackle and coming to 'osses, I find that Sir Charles John Darling, Kt., is the son of Charles Darling, of Langham Hall, Essex. Born on a cold December morning in the 40's, he was called to the Bar in 1874 and took silk in 1885. He has been a Judge of the King's Bench Division of the High Court of Justice since 1897. He married Mary, daughter of Major-General Wilberforce Harris Greathed, C.B., in 1885, and no doubt as a diversion from matrimony sat in Parliament as Member for Deptford from 1888 to 1897, in which latter year, as we have seen, he was made Judge.

Mr. Justice Darling has in his time published three books, namely, "Scintillae Juris," "Meditations in the Tea Room," and "Seria Ludo." They are good, readable books, though a trifle academic, and lawyers chortle over them. Brevity and point are the chief characteristics of the contents. Some of Sir Charles' epigrams are most piquant. "Order 14 is Heaven's first law" is one of them, and perhaps the best.

But apparently Mr. Justice Darling is not writing any more; for, according to "Who's Who," his recreations now are "hunting and painting." Before the ribald smile at the "painting" they must please recollect that the Lord Chief Justice of England himself sings glees.

It is only necessary to add that Sir Charles Darling is a member of the Carlton, Athenaeum, and Burlington Fine Art Clubs, and that he is known affectionately to his intimates by the pet name - "Darling."

"Judicial Light Weight"

HENRY FIELDING DICKENS

"HIS FATHER INVENTED PICKWICK"   **13th May 1897**

Parentage:

Born: 16th January 1849, the sixth son of Charles Dickens, the novelist, and Catherine Thompson, eldest daughter of George Hogarth, music and drama critic.

Educated:

Wimbledon School (kept by Messrs. Brackenbury and Wynn) and Trinity Hall, Cambridge. Graduated B.A. and 29th Wrangler in the Mathematics Tripos (1872).

Career:

Professional:

1873 - Called to the Bar of the Inner Temple.

1892 - Queen's Counsel.

1892 - 1918 - Recorder of Maidstone.

1899 - Bencher of the Inner Temple.

1917 - 1932 - Common Serjeant of the City of London.

1922 - Knighted.

Personal:

1876 - Married Marie, daughter of M. Antonin Roche. Three sons and three daughters.

Died:

31st December 1933.

Henry Dickens was the sixth son of Charles Dickens, the famous novelist. Henry Dickens practised on the Home Circuit and at Maidstone Sessions, being one time Recorder of Deal and later Maidstone itself. His father had been very fond of Kent and spent much time there.

It is as Common Serjeant of the City of London that he is best remembered, a post he held for 15 years, retiring in his 83rd year. The Common Serjeant is appointed by the Crown and, along with the Recorder and the Commissioner, was one of the permanent judges at the Old Bailey.

A contemporary Recorder, Sir Thomas Wild, K.C., said of him: "He modelled his conduct on true Dickensian principles which had done so much for progress, humanity and liberty". He is believed to have been one of the last judges always to use a quill pen at The Old Bailey.

His daughter, Monica Dickens, is an eminent novelist and still writing.

MR. HENRY FIELDING DICKENS, Q.C.

THE fifth surviving son of the Inventor of Pickwick, he was born seven-and-forty years ago; and, having been made a Bachelor of Arts, he was called to the Bar by the Honourable Society of the Inner Temple. He began to practise in the South-Eastern Counties, where his father's name was one to conjure with; and finding, in the fulness of time, that Kent and Sussex were growing tired of Mr. Willis, he ventured to take silk. The venture was wise; for he has since gotten a substantial and steadily increasing practice as a leader. He has been Recorder of Deal, and he is now Recorder of Maidstone; which is in the very centre of the country of Pickwick. He is a very painstaking, cheerful advocate; yet with all his merit he owes a good deal to the fact that he is the son of a popular idol.

He is an industrious and pleasant gentleman who has no particular history at the Bar.

"His father invented Pickwick"

EDWARD STRATHEARN GORDON
(Baron Gordon of Drumearn)

Parentage:
Born: 10th April 1814 at Inverness, eldest son of John Gordon, Major 2nd Regiment and Catherine, daughter of Alexander Smith.

Educated:
Royal Academy, Inverness and University of Edinburgh. Took LL.B. from both Glasgow and Edinburgh Universities.

Career:
Professional:
1835 - Called to the Bar.
1858 - 1866 - Sheriff of Perthshire and Advocate-Depute.
1866 - 1867 - Solicitor-General for Scotland.
1867 - 1868 - Lord Advocate.
1868 - Queen's Counsel.
1868 - 1874 - Dean of Faculty by unanimous election.
1874 - 1876 - Lord Advocate.
1874 - Gazetted as Privy Counsellor.
October 1876 - Created a Lord of Appeal in Ordinary with the style and title of Baron Gordon of Drumearn. Sat until July 1879.

Political:
December 1867 - November 1868 - Conservative M.P. for Thetford, Norfolk until borough disenfranchised.
1868 - Unsuccessfully contested Glasgow and Aberdeen University Seat.
1869 - Elected M.P. for Glasgow and Aberdeen Universities at by-election caused by Rt. Hon. James Moncreiff's appointment as Lord of Session.

General:
1859 - Captain of the Advocates' Volunteer Battalion and later Colonel 1st Edinburgh Battalion.

Personal:
1845 - Married Agnes, only child of James McInnes of Auchenreoch, Stirlingshire.

Died:
21st August 1879 at Brussels.

Edward Gordon was not only a leading Scottish lawyer, but heavily involved in the politics of the Calvinist Church in Scotland. Although a staunch Calvinist, Gordon still supported the established Church of Scotland on the matter of patronage, which resulted in the Free Church Secession.

He stood for Parliament as a Conservative, contesting the University seat of Aberdeen and Glasgow in 1868. His opponent was the Right Honourable James Moncrieff, who stood in the Liberal interest and who was also a Lord Advocate and future Lord Justice-Clerk. Gordon received 2020 votes against Moncrieff's 2067. The following year in a by-election on Moncrieff's elevation to the Bench, Gordon was returned to Parliament for the same seat.

He died a very rich man, having earned one large fortune through his practice and received another on his marriage. On his appointment as Law Lord he was granted a salary of £6,000 a year when income tax was 2d. in the pound.

His most famous case was the Yelverton Marriage, Yelverton v. Longworth [(1864) 10 Jur. NS 1209 HL]

THE RIGHT HONOURABLE
EDWARD STRATHEARN GORDON

WHEN the present Government came into office they looked around for a Scotchman and a Conservative of ability and learning in order to make of him a Lord Advocate. Failing to find such a person they made a Lord Advocate of Mr. Gordon. And Mr. Gordon has displayed many qualities useful in such a post. Scotch law is so great a mystery that it matters little whether he is learned in it; Scotch religion is an important force, and in that he is known to be painfully orthodox. Moreover he has not that fatal gift of cynicism and brilliancy which made his predecessor remarkable, and although extremely pious, he is courteous, amiable, and claims kinship with the Covenanters. During the sixty years that he has lived he has followed the law with patience, won promotion with regularity, and never swerved from the paths of respectability. Successively a Queen's Counsel, a Sheriff, and a Scotch Solicitor-General, he is now for the second time in the post he occupies. He introduced the Bill to regulate Church Patronage in Scotland, and has earned by it as much popularity as criticism; but it will never be forgotten that he is the Lieutenant-Colonel of the Queen's City of Edinburgh Rifle Volunteers.

"Lord Advocate"

HENRY HAWKINS
(Baron Brampton)

"THE TICHBORNE CASE"   **21st June 1873**

Parentage:
Born: 14th September 1817, son of John Hawkins "Family" solicitor and Susanna, daughter of Theed Pearse, Clerk of the Peace for Bedfordshire.

Educated:
Bedford School

Professional:
Employed in father's office.
1839 - Entered Middle Temple.
1843 - Called to the Bar.
1858 - Queen's Counsel.
1876 - Appointed a Judge of the Queen's Bench Division of the High Court of Justice and almost immediately transferred to the Exchequer Division. Knighted.
1880 - The Exchequer Division absorbed by the Queen's Bench Division.
1898 - Resigned and sworn of the Privy Council.
August 1899 - Created Baron Brampton of Brampton in the County of Huntingdon. Sat in House of Lords until August 1902.

Political:
1865 - Contested Barnstaple in the Liberal interest.

General:
1878 - Honorary Member of the Jockey Club.

Personal:
Twice married. His second wife was Jane Louise, daughter of H.F. Reynolds of Holme. No children of either union.

Died:
6th October 1907 at his house in Tilney Street and buried in Kensal Green Cemetery.

Harry Hawkins came from a prosperous middle-class family in Bedfordshire and having been called to the Bar in 1843 his progress was not rapid, but unbroken. He obtained a great reputation as a fighting advocate and a skilful cross-examiner.

He appeared mainly in criminal cases, notably as one of the Counsel for the Defendant in the Tichborne Ejectment Actions. He also led for the Crown in the prosecution of the claimant (Orton or Castro) before Cockburn, C.J. (q.v.) in which his opening speech lasted six days and his reply nine days.

As a Judge he presided over the trial of the Stauntons for murder; a particularly gruesome case involving starving a woman to death. He was affectionately nicknamed "Hanging Hawkins".

He was elected an Honorary Member of the Jockey Club, but although fond of racing he never owned horses himself. After his retirement he was converted to Catholicism and he and his wife presented the Chapel of St. Augustine and St. Gregory in Westminster Cathedral.

MR. HENRY HAWKINS, Q.C.

DURING the thirty years that he has been an advocate, Mr. Hawkins has made for himself as such a first-rate reputation. He is not an orator in the high-flown sense, and it was commonly supposed that he did not know how to deal with a hostile witness until his cross-examination of Mr. Baigent became famous. He was declared also not to work at his briefs, until his masterly and most proper summary of the Tichborne case brought him into favourable comparison with Sir John Coleridge, and proved that he had spent his days and nights over an overwhelming mass of evidence. Yet it has always been found that he had a knack of winning verdicts against the heaviest odds. He is very quick at seeing the weakness of his opponent, quicker perhaps than in marshalling his own forces, and when before the enemy has often been known to attempt fine strokes in generalship. Withal he has the drollest and most irresistible manner, and the hoarsest voice extant, which latter gift of nature he is once said to have declared was worth £5000 a-year to him; and when he undertakes to tickle a witness, to talk at a doubtful juror, or even to out-manoeuvre the sacred Bench itself, it is not without chances of success and the certainty of making a good retreat in case of failure. With these qualities he has naturally been engaged in some of the greatest trials that have been held of late years - so that the cases of Roupell, of Strahan Paul and Bates, of the Sun Fire Office, and of Saurin v. Starr are all associated with his name. He once was fond of horse-racing and of the fair sex; but he has long ceased to study the minor prophets, and merely rides now for the sake of his health, on a horse well known to the early frequenters of Rotten Row; while he has proved, when sitting in the Crown Court, that he can be as serious as any occasion demands. Being as he is an undeniably well-read and sound lawyer, and having been now long in the front rank of his profession, it has been matter of surprise to many that he has not been made a Judge, all the more that the fact of his picking his briefs proves him to be rich enough to enjoy that luxury were it offered to him. Possibly one reason may be that he has never secured the opportunity of serving any Party in Parliament, for although he offered himself to the electors of Barnstaple eight years ago, he was defeated, and has not since tempted Providence in that way.

"The Tichborne case"

RUFUS DANIEL ISAACS
(The Marquis of Reading)

Parentage:

Born: 10th October 1860 at 3 Bury Street in the Parish of St. Mary Axe, London, second son and fourth child of Joseph Michael Isaacs, fruit merchant of Spitalfields and Sarah, daughter of Daniel Davis of London; great-nephew of Daniel Mendoza the prize-fighter.

Educated:

M. Kahn's school, Brussels, Mr. Mendes's Anglo-Jewish School, Northwick Terrace, Regent's Park and University College School, Gower Street, leaving July 1874.

Career:

Early:

1875 - Apprenticed to M. Isaacs & Sons, fruit merchants and ship-brokers.

October 1876 - September 1877 - Ship's boy aboard "Blair Athole".

November 1879 - Member of the Stock Exchange. Jobber in the foreign market.

August 1884 - "Hammered" as unable to meet his obligations - £8,000.

Professional:

1885 - Entered the Middle Temple.

1887 - Called to the Bar.

April 1898 - Queen's Counsel.

1905 - Bencher of the Middle Temple.

March 1910 - Solicitor-General and Knighted.

October 1910 - Attorney-General.

July 1911 - Sworn of the Privy Council, K.C.V.O.

October 1913 - Lord Chief Justice of England.

1914 - Created Baron Reading of Erleigh in the County of Berkshire.

1916 - Created Viscount Erleigh.

1917 - Created Earl Reading.

1921 - Resigns as Lord Chief Justice.

1927 - Treasurer of the Middle Temple.

Political:

1900 - Contested North Kensington.

August 1904 - October 1913 - M.P. for Reading.

September 1915 - Led Anglo-French Mission to U.S.A. to raise credits. Appointed K.C.B.

April 1917 - High Commissioner to U.S.A. and Canada.

January - July 1918 - Ambassador to the U.S.A.

January 1921 - Viceroy and Governor General of India. Created G.C.S.I. and G.C.I.E.

1922 - Created G.C.V.O.

April 1926 - Retired as Viceroy. Created Marquis of Reading.

August - October 1931 - Foreign Secretary.

Personal:

1887 - Married (1) Alice Edith, third daughter of Albert Cohen of Hampstead (d. 1930). (2) In 1931 Stella, third daughter of Charles Charnaud. One son - Gerald Rufus born 1889.

Died:

30th December 1935 at Curzon Street. Cremated at Golders Green.

Rufus Isaacs was one of the great achievers in the first half of the 20th Century. His achievements are made even more remarkable by the financial scandals which surrounded his career. Aged 19 he falsified his age to become a jobber on the Stock Exchange and five years afterwards was hammered with debts of £8,000. He decided to repair his fortunes at the Bar where his knowledge of shady financial dealings stood him in good stead in the recently established Commercial Court.

In 1910 he was appointed Attorney-General and sworn of the Privy Council and in 1911 was made a K.C.V.O., in the Sovereign's personal gift, for his handling of the prosecution of Mylius who accused George V of bigamy [R.v. Mylius - The Times, 2nd Feb. 1911]. The next year he was involved in insider dealing in Marconi shares along with Lloyd George, the Chancellor of the Exchequer and Herbert Samuel, the Postmaster General. He avoided Censure as the House voted purely on party lines. As a reward he was appointed Lord Chief Justice. After the War, during which he served as British Ambassador in the U.S.A. while still Lord Chief Justice, he resigned the position to become Viceroy of India and later Foreign Secretary.

As Lord Chief Justice he presided at the trial of Sir Roger Casement for High Treason in which F.E. Smith (q.v.) led for the Crown [R.v. Casement - 1917, 1K.B., 98.].

MR. RUFUS DANIEL ISAACS, K.C., M.P.

HIS father, a merchant in the City of London, gave him a good education at University College School, and he became a man of the world by acquiring larger knowledge in Brussels and in Hanover. He is only four-and-forty, but he is full of brains, and he has seen a good deal of life. It is said that he first went to sea; but presently he returned, to business, and he has never been "at sea" since. His abilities, however, were too great for ordinary business, so he tried the Stock Exchange, and found that its walls limited his ambitions. Finally he learned his true vocation as an Advocate; for he is now at the top of his profession, having gained the dizzy eminence at a very early age by sheer hard work and real merit. For he has the unusual combination of great brain power with invincible endurance; for in his younger days he was an adept at boxing, while he still keeps himself "fit" by riding, cycling, and golfing. Thus he is still well able to take a great deal of physical as well as legal beating; being one of those who never give in while he has a leg left to stand upon. He is naturally at his best in a commercial, or Stock Exchange case; for of such he knows all the ropes. Nevertheless his fame brings him big briefs in sensational and fashionable cases of all kinds; in which he makes no mistakes. He does not try to be brilliant; he has a quiet and very convincing way with him, and altogether, with the single exception of Sir Edward Clarke, he is recognised as the leader of the Common Law Bar.

Socially, he is quite popular; for not only is he exceedingly clever, rather good-looking, and very good-tempered, but he is absolutely devoid of conceit.

"Rufus"

GEORGE JESSEL

"THE LAW"   \text{\textbf{1st March 1879}}

Parentage:
Born: 13th February 1824 in London, youngest son of Zadok Aaron Jessel of Savile Row and Putney, a substantial merchant.

Educated:
Mr. Neumegen's School for Jews at Kew and University College, London. 1840 Matriculated. 1843 Graduated B.A. with honours in Mathematics, Natural Philosophy, Vegetable Physiology and Structural Botany with prizes in the two last subjects. 1844 Proceeded M.A. with the gold medal in Mathematics and Natural Philosophy. 1846 Elected fellow of University College.

Career:
Professional:
1842 - Entered Lincoln's Inn.
1847 - Called to the Bar of Lincoln's Inn.
1861 - Refused silk by Lord Westbury L.C.
1865 - Queen's Counsel.
1865 - Elected Bencher of Lincoln's Inn.
1871 - Solicitor-General.
1873 - Appointed Master of the Rolls, sworn of the Privy Council. Died in office.
1883 - Treasurer of Lincoln's Inn.

Political:
December 1868 - Elected M.P. for Dover in the Liberal interest. He resigned on his appointment as Master of the Rolls although not obliged to do so.

General:
1862 - Senator of London University.
1881 - 1883 - Vice-Chancellor of London University.
Prepared the Brown Institute Committee's Report on the treatment of diseases and injuries to animals.
1881 - Member of the Royal Commission to enquire into the workings of the Medical Acts and was mainly responsible for its report.
Vice-President of the Council for Legal Education. Fellow of the Royal Society. He retained his interest in botany to the last.

Personal:
1856 - Married Amelia, eldest daughter of Joseph Moses of London. Left two sons and three daughters.

Died:
21st March 1883 at London and buried at the Cemetery of the United Synagogue at Willesden.

A graduate of the University of London where he was a most distinguished student of botany and where he obtained a fellowship at University College, Jessel read for the Bar at Lincoln's Inn and practised both as a conveyancer and in the Rolls Court.

He became M.P. for Dover and in Parliament is said to have attracted the notice of Mr. Gladstone by his speech on the Bankruptcy Bill of 1869. He was raised to the Bench as Master of the Rolls in the same year in which the Judicature Act was passed which transformed the Court system. Under the Acts of 1873 and amending Act of 1875 the Master of the Rolls remained a judge in the first instance, became the Ordinary President of the Court of Appeal in Chancery cases and a member of the Rules Committee. This was in addition to being the working head of the Patent Office.

The Act of 1881 relieved Jessel of his duties at first instance much against his will. His most important judgment was in the case of Walsh v. Lonsdale [(1882), 21 Ch.D.9] concerning the union of law and equity effected by the Judicature Act.

He never reserved judgment in the Rolls Court and only twice in the Court of Appeal and that at the request of his fellow judges. His most famous saying was: "I may be wrong, and I sometimes am, but I never doubt."

THE RIGHT HON. SIR GEORGE JESSEL

MR. ZACHARIAH JESSEL, a diamond merchant, of Saville Row, was blessed five and fifty years ago with a son. This son he sent to University College, London, and thence to the Bar. The young man was very industrious and very able; he soon mastered the whole of the law of Real Estate; he became well known as a successful pleader; he was made a Queen's Counsel and a Bencher of his Inn; and in 1871, while yet under fifty, he was appointed Solicitor-General by Mr. Gladstone. In 1873 he was still further elevated by being appointed Master of the Rolls; and in 1875 he became a Judge of the Supreme Court of Judicature, being the first Jew ever appointed to the Judicial Bench in England. He is what is called a strong Judge; he conducts his business in the most admirable manner and with the most perfect taste; and he is not only very learned in the law, but very sound and very just in his decisions. Personally he is very popular, much admired, and greatly respected; and he owes all he is, and nearly all he has, to his own great natural talents, untiring industry, and undoubted honesty.

"The Law"

FITZ ROY KELLY

"THE LORD CHIEF BARON"   **4th November 1871**

Parentage:
Born: October 1796 in London, son of Captain Robert Hawke Kelly R.N., son of Colonel Robert Kelly of the East India Company's Service, and Isabella, daughter of Captain Fordyce, carver and cupbearer to H.M. King George III.

Educated:
Mr. Farrer's School, Chelsea.

Career:
Professional:
Office of Mr. Brutton, solicitor of Bethnal Green.
1817 - Entered Lincoln's Inn.
1824 - Called to the Bar of Lincoln's Inn.
1834 - King's Counsel.
1839 - Bencher of Lincoln's Inn.
June 1845 - July 1846 - Solicitor-General. Knighted.
February 1852 - December 1852 - Solicitor-General.
February 1858 - June 1859 - Attorney-General.
July 1866 - Lord Chief Baron of the Court of Exchequer and sworn of the Privy Council. Died in office.

Political:
1830 - Contested Hythe unsuccessfully at the General Election.
1832 - Contested Ipswich unsuccessfully.
1835 - Returned for Ipswich but unseated on petition.
1837 - Contested Ipswich at the General Election, defeated by a few votes, claimed a scrutiny and won the seat.
1841 - Lost Ipswich at the General Election.
1843 - Returned for the Borough of Cambridge.
1847 - Did not seek re-election for the Borough of Cambridge, but instead unsuccessfully contested Lyme Regis.
April 1852 - Elected M.P. for Harwich but before taking his seat a vacancy occurred for the Eastern Division of Suffolk where he had large estates at Sproughton near Ipswich.
May 1852 - Elected M.P. for East Suffolk which he held until elevated to the Bench.

Personal:
1821 - Married (1) Agnes Scarth, daughter of Captain Mason of Leith. (2) in 1856 Ada, daughter of Mark Cunningham of Boyle, County Roscommon. Four daughters.

Died:
18th September 1880 at Brighton. Buried at Highgate.

Fitz Roy Kelly came from an old-established East India Company family and the Company were to promote his early career at the Bar. Prior to the Judicature Act 1873 there were three Common Law Courts, the Queen's Bench, Common Pleas and Exchequer. The Head of the Court of Exchequer bore the title of Lord Chief Baron and the Judges of the Court were known as "Mr. Baron___". Kelly deplored the change of style and the subsequent suppression of the Exchequer Division which was merged with the Queen's Bench. Normally the Lord Chief Baron was made a peer on appointment or retirement, but Fitz Roy Kelly was passed over due to his disclosure that the judgment of the Judicial Committee of the Privy Council in the case of Risdale was not unanimous.

After only one year on the Home Circuit he joined the Norfolk Circuit where he built up an excellent practice and became Standing Counsel to the Bank of England and the East India Company. When Attorney-General his income at the Bar, particularly in the House of Lords and before the Privy Council, was reported to be in excess of £25,000 a year. Taking a multiple of 60 this would give him an income of £1.5 million a year in today's money.

His political career was dubious to say the least - he was unseated on petition on one occasion and displaced the sitting member on a scrutiny two years afterwards.

He defended Frost, the Chartist, in the trial for High Treason arising out of the riots at Newport, Monmouthshire and saved his life [R.v. Frost 4 St. Tr. (N.S.) 85]. He successfully prosecuted the former Tractarian leader and future Cardinal John Henry Newman for criminal libel [R.v. Newman (1853) 1 E&B 558].

THE RIGHT HON. SIR FITZ ROY EDWARD KELLY

IN a country where, as in England, the political, social, and religious systems are so closely interwoven that a capability of satisfying the requirements of all is necessary to success in either of them, it necessarily happens that the best men in each department are not usually to be found in the foremost positions. We are continually compelled to accept in Politics the worse politician because he makes the better social figure; in Theology the worse theologian because he is the better politician; in Law the worse lawyer because he is the better religionist. The happy combination of pre-eminence in one department and of sufficient superiority in all is so seldom found, that some of the most remarkable men modern England has produced are by the fatal necessity of the situation precluded from serving their country in those highest positions which best befit them.

Such has been the case with Sir Fitz Roy Kelly. Born seventy-five years ago, he was destined from an early age for the Bar; and as soon as he had won for himself a hearing, he gave the promise, which he has since richly fulfilled, of that clear intellect, great ability, and conscientious industry which entitle him to rank among the very first lawyers of the country. As an advocate he has achieved the most brilliant successes. He saved a Chartist from the extreme penalty of high treason, and he won for their possessors the vast Bridgwater estates and the premier earldoms of England, Ireland, and Scotland; having in two of the cases for supporter, and in one for opponent, that Mr. Bethell who was perhaps his only equal. He has taken also a most active part in the consolidation of the Statute Law; he proposed, and finally succeeded in effecting, one of the greatest of our modern law reforms, in the abolition of capital punishment for all offences save those of murder and high treason; and one of his latest achievements in Parliament was a masterly advocacy of the claims of the Nawab of the Carnatic. Endowed with parts which he had sedulously cultivated, blessed by Nature with a fitting presence, and distinguished by the courteous demeanour which commonly accompanies a sense of superiority, he seemed certainly destined to attain to that woolsack which should be the seat of the highest legal ability.

That political life which is the necessary stepping-stone to such a dignity betrayed, however, the just expectation that might have been founded upon it. Returned for Ipswich in 1835, he had to meet a petition which unseated him, and when defending himself a charge was made against him of an irregularity in proceeding, the memory of which has ever since been a stumbling-block in his career. Two years later he succeeded in making good his claim to a seat in the House of Commons, and soon became in succession Solicitor-General and Attorney-General; but John Pilgrim was never forgotten, and Mr. Kelly was long passed over and relegated to a comparative obscurity, which his worth rendered all the more remarkable. At last he was called, five years ago, to that position of Lord Chief Baron of the Court of Exchequer which he now so admirably fills, and in which he compels the recognition by all men of his power and rectitude.

"The Lord Chief Baron."

ROBERT MALCOLM KERR

"THE CITY OF LONDON COURT" **22nd November 1900**

Parentage:
Born: 1821 at Glasgow.

Educated:
Glasgow University.

Career:
Professional:
Writer to the Signet and Commissary-Depute of Hamilton and Campsie.
1843 - Called to the Scottish Bar.
1848 - Called to the Bar of Lincoln's Inn.
1859 - 1901 - Judge of the City of London Court.

General:
1897 - 1898 - Master of the Tallow-Chandlers Company.
Lieutenant for the City of London.

Died:
21st November 1902.

Robert Kerr, commonly called "The Commissioner", had a very long reign at The Old Bailey from 1859 to 1901. He was born in Glasgow, came from merchant stock and was a member of both the Scottish and English Bars. As can be seen from the excellent cartoon of him, he was a cantankerous lawyer who lacked polish.

Although he never lost his Scottishness, he was very popular in the City itself and became Master of the Tallow-Chandlers Company in the year 1897/1898.

The most famous story about him involved an unfortunate barrister by the name of Warburton Pyke who was asked by the Commissioner:

"What d'ye call yersel' War-r-rburt-rton Pyke forr?"

Warburton-Pyke: "Because it's my name - and I use it; but may I ask you why you call yourself Car when you are a Cur?"

MR. COMMISSIONER KERR

A WRITER to the Signet (who was also Commissary Depute of Hamilton and Campsie) became his father seventy-nine years ago; and, his mother being daughter of a Glasgow merchant named Malcolm, Robert Malcolm Kerr was very Scotch, and went to Glasgow University (where he was eventually made a Doctor of Laws). He married, became a Scotch Advocate, and, five years later, a Barrister of Lincoln's Inn. Then, as Deputy Judge of County Courts, he found Scotland a good place to live out of; and, later, as Judge of the Old Sheriffs' Court, he naturally fitted the new City of London Court, over which he has now presided for so many years. He is also a Commissioner of the Central Criminal Court, and he has been a Master of the Tallow-Chandlers' Company without softening the asperities of his character. He is chiefly famous for his wide acquaintance with Blackstone's "Commentaries on the Laws of England," and the unique way in which he applies those laws; but though he has been guilty of several valuable legal works, he has twice failed to get into Parliament. He is a shrewd fellow who holds the best paid Office in all the inferior Courts of England; though why the City of London should have preferred a Scotchman, and why such a Scotchman, no living man can perceive through the mists of antiquity that now veil the beginning of his judgment. Nevertheless, he administers a kind of rough and ready justice that irritates many and pleases a few. His worst faults are his inclination to decide cases when only part heard and his occasional disregard of the existing state of the Law; and his greatest virtue is his wholesomeness in keeping down costs and arrears of work. For years he has successfully defied the High Court by persisting in his refusal to trouble himself by taking notes of his cases. The City Authorities have offered him a very large pension, but he has resisted all their temptations by sitting tight where he is. He is not always gracious to Counsel; he does not believe in juries, and it is his special delight to ridicule the Mayor's Court which sits over the way.

He is undeniably a humourist of the caustic kind; yet he has friends.

"the City of London Court"

ALFRED TRISTRAM LAWRENCE
(Baron Trevethin)

Parentage:
Born: 24th November 1843 at Pontypool, the eldest son of David Lawrence, surgeon of Pontypool and Elizabeth, daughter of Charles Morgan Williams.

Educated:
Mill Hill School and Trinity Hall, Cambridge. Placed second in the First Class of the Law Tripos 1866.

Career:
Professional:
1869 - Called to the Bar of the Middle Temple.
1882 - Junior Counsel to the Admiralty.
1885 - Recorder of Windsor.
1897 - Queen's Counsel.
1904 - Appointed Judge of the Queen's Bench Division of the High Court of Justice. Elected Bencher of the Middle Temple.
1914 - Treasurer of the Middle Temple.
April 1921 - Appointed Lord Chief Justice of England, sworn of the Privy Council and created Baron Trevethin of Blaengawney in the County of Monmouth.
March 1922 - Resigned.

General:
A keen hunter and rider in point-to-point races and steeplechasing. A golfer and angler.

Personal:
1875 - Married his cousin, Jessie Elizabeth, daughter of George Lawrence of Moreton Court near Hereford, sister of Sir Walter Lawrence. His eldest son, Alfred Clive, became Treasury Solicitor and Queen's Proctor. His third son, Geoffrey, was appointed a Judge of the Queen's Bench Division of the High Court of Justice in 1932, Lord Justice of Appeal (1945), presided over the trial of the War Criminals at Nuremberg and was created Baron Oaksey and a Lord of Appeal in Ordinary in 1947. His grandson is the television racing personality "John Lawrence (Oaksey)".

Died:
3rd August 1936 fishing in the Wye above Builth Wells, aged 92.

The family of Lorry Lawrence are now as well known for their exploits with horses as they are distinguished in law. A sound lawyer, Lawrence enjoyed a busy and varied practice both on the circuit and in London and a combination of natural diffidence and family responsibilities caused him to delay taking silk until his 54th year and after 28 years as a junior.

Lloyd George, the then Prime Minister, persuaded Lord Reading (q.v.) to accept the post of Viceroy of India, necessitating his resignation as Lord Chief Justice: The Attorney-General, Sir Gordon Hewart, would normally have become Lord Chief Justice but Lloyd George needed to retain him in the Cabinet and so appointed Lorry as a stopgap Lord Chief Justice, having first obtained an undated letter of resignation from him. When Hewart wished to take up the position of Lord Chief Justice a year later, Lorry learned about his resignation from the post on reading the daily newspapers.

Despite Lorry's age, Lloyd George's caution was not unfounded as he lived to the age of 92 and only died as a result of falling into the Wye whilst fishing.

He and Lord Reading appeared as Junior Counsel for Sir George Chetwynd, Bart., in his famous libel action against Lord Durham, a Steward of the Jockey Club, and which the Court referred to arbitration before three Stewards of the Jockey Club. He presided over the libel action brought by Lloyd George as Chancellor of the Exchequer against *The People* newspaper, in which Rufus Isaacs (q.v.) led for the Plaintiff and Sir Edward Carson (q.v.) for the Defendants.

THE HONOURABLE SIR ALFRED TRISTRAM LAWRENCE

B ORN four-and-sixty years ago, Sir Alfred Tristram Lawrence passed an industrious boyhood and a painstaking youth; and the result of his pains and labour was a First in Law, at Trinity Hall, Cambridge. He is not "Long John". Nay: "Long John" is his judicial brother, Sir John Compton Lawrence.

Leaving Cambridge, he ate his dinners at the Middle Temple, and was called to the Bar in June, 1869. He joined the Oxford Circuit, and after a while became known as a thoroughly trustworthy counsel, who, if dogged, pertinacious work could do it, would do his best for his clients. He had joined the longest winded of the Circuits, yet was himself a man of few words and many thoughts, so that to distinguish him from the other two Alfreds - Alfred Young and Alfred Lyttelton - he was called "The Judicious Alfred." His words were not only few but also deliberate, which in his case was no mark of intellectual sluggishness, for what they lost in haste they gained in point. His slowness of utterance was the natural result of his passion for caution and exactitude. That was why he always won the ear of the Court.

For twenty-eight years after he was called to the Bar he wore a stuff gown; and when, in 1897, he took silk, he became an excellent leader, especially in commercial cases. He was appointed Commissioner of Assizes of the North-Eastern Circuit, and Recorder of Windsor; and in 1904 he was made a Judge of the High Court - not only an excellent, but also a most popular appointment.

A Welshman hailing from Scotland, he has displayed on the Bench a matter-of-fact style of speech and the demeanour of a sphinx, the true judicial demeanour. Though he has a keen, cymric sense of humour, he does not in his judicial capacity encourage facetiousness in others; and he is never facetious himself. His shining judicial quality is an extraordinary patience. He has had need of it. One of his first acts on his elevation to the Bench was to preside for thirty days over the trial of Ernest Terah Hooley. In that trial he exhibited a patience which Job never equalled, and the late Lord Brampton never surpassed.

Off the Bench Sir Alfred Tristram Lawrence is a thoroughly good sportsman; and his friends call him "Lorry". He is nowadays a keen golfer and a keen shot. In his younger days he was a first-class light-weight across country; and we have reason to believe that he often figured between the flags as a steeplechase-rider.

"Lorry"

GEORGE HENRY LEWIS

"AN ASTUTE LAWYER"   **2nd September 1876**

Parentage:
Born: 21st April 1833 at 10 Ely Place, Holborn, second son of James Graham Lewis, solicitor and Harriet, daughter of Henry Davis of London.

Educated:
At a private Jewish School in Edmonton and at University College, London.

Career:
Professional:
1851 - Articled to his father.
1856 - Admitted a solicitor. Joined Lewis & Lewis of which his father and uncle, George Lewis, were the only partners.
1892 - Knighted.
1902 - Baronet.
1905 - C.V.O.

Personal:
1863 - Married (1) Victorine, daughter of Philip Kann of Frankfurt-am-Mainz (d. 1865). One daughter. (2) in 1867 Elizabeth, daughter of Ferdinand Eberstadbt of Mannheim. Had two daughters and one son, George James Graham, 2nd Bart. and Senior Partner of Lewis & Lewis.

Died:
7th December 1911 at 88 Portland Place, London and buried in the Jewish Cemetery, Willesden.

George Lewis was born "over the shop" at 10 Ely Place which housed the solicitors' partnership of Lewis & Lewis, a partnership between his father and uncle. The practice might have served as the model of that of Mr. Jagger's in Dickens' book *Great Expectations* dealing mainly with criminal, fraud and bankruptcy cases. It also had a long standing connection with the theatre.

He had an unrivalled knowledge of "the skeletons in the cupboard" of almost everyone in society and was thus frequently able to secure a settlement in his cases by the threat of unwelcome revelations at the trial if the action proceeded. He was a friend of the Prince of Wales, later King Edward VII, and acted in many cases involving members of The Marlborough House Set.

His early practice was in the Magistrates Courts and he gained much notoriety in the case brought by Dr. Thorn against Overend, Gurney and Co. He instructed Charles Russell (q.v.) before the Parnell Commission.

MR. GEORGE HENRY LEWIS

NEARLY sixty years ago there was established in Ely Place a firm of solicitors, to which twenty years ago there was admitted young George Lewis, then a lad of twenty-three, and the son of the firm's original founder. The new junior partner was a smart lad, who had received a so-called education as a student of University College, London, and who had given himself a real education as a student of human nature. He rapidly made himself a master of the technicalities of the attorney's profession, and soon disclosed capabilities of dealing with them in such a way as should make a solicitor a more important person than had hitherto been held to be possible. For his notion was to succeed in every case at any price, and to give to the client the advice that would free him of his difficulties at any rate; so that in course of time it came to be known that in Ely Place there was a helpful firm which generally got the better of the adversary. Of this firm George Lewis, now a man of three and forty, was and is the peculiar ornament, and accordingly it has been found that those who mean to win are well-advised to put their case, whatever it may be, in his hands. He is indeed an astute lawyer, of aspirations not bounded by the ordinary professional limits. He delights to conduct a case himself in all courts in which a solicitor is admitted to practise; and in such courts he has again and again encountered and signally overthrown some of the greatest luminaries of the Bar. In matters of finance and speculation he is especially competent, for he is believed to know enough to hang half the people in the City, and there are, consequently, few of them who can stand up undismayed against his cross-examination. In the case of Overend, Gurney, and Co., of Barned's Banking Company, of the Ottoman and Symrna Railway Company, and of the scuttling of the *Severn*, he showed himself a master of the City sciences; besides which he has acquired a considerable reputation as a manager of journalistic cases. He has thus acquired for his firm a distinct position as the defenders of the unwary; and besides being the solicitor to three daily and to several weekly newspapers, he is also the permanent official adviser of Lloyd's Salvage Association, of the Stock Exchange in its private windings-up of defaulting members, of the Charity Organisation Society, and of the Dramatic Authors' Society.

Mr. Lewis is, in addition to all this, very largely consulted by members of his own profession in delicate matters which never see the light, and he has recently distinguished himself during the inquiry into the death of Mr. Bravo in a manner not likely to be forgotten. He has a considerable acquaintance among persons connected with finance, journalism, and the theatres, and any such who find themselves in legal trouble could probably not find a better guide than him to a haven of safety through the technicalities of the law and the dispositions of magistrates and jurymen. On the whole, he is a remarkable instance of the manner in which the much-lauded distinction acts that is still kept up between barristers and solicitors, to the prejudice of solicitors.

"An astute lawyer"

CHARLES WILLIE MATHEWS

"HE CAN MARSHALL EVIDENCE"   **6th February 1892**

Parentage:
Born: 16th October 1850 in New York, the son of William and Elizabeth West. His mother, who was an actress at Burton's Theatre, (stage name Lizzie Weston) married, secondly, A.H. Davenport, an actor and, thirdly, as his second wife, Charles James Mathews, actor and dramatist. He assumed his second stepfather's name by deed poll.

Educated:
Eton.

Career:
Professional:
1872 - Called to the Bar of the Middle Temple.
1886 - Appointed one of the two Junior Treasury Counsel at the Central Criminal Court.
1888 - Appointed one of the three Senior Treasury Counsel.
1893 - Recorder of Salisbury.
1901 - Elected a Bencher of the Middle Temple.
1907 - Knighted on the occasion of the opening of the new Central Criminal Court by the King.
1908 - Appointed Director of Public Prosecutions and held office until his death.
1911 - K.C.B.
1917 - Baronet.

Political:
1892 - Contested Winchester in the Liberal interest.

General:
Fond of riding and race meetings. Member of the Turf, Garrick and Beefsteak Clubs.

Personal:
1888 - Married Lucy, daughter of Lindsay Sloper, musician. No issue.

Died:
6th June 1920 at London.

Charles Mathews' real name was West, although early on in life he assumed his stepfather's name of Mathews, and came of a theatrical background. Leaving school he went straight to the Bar and read in the chambers of Montagu Williams, a well-known criminal lawyer, and was called before his 22nd birthday, a very early age, especially for the 19th Century.

He practised mainly at The Old Bailey and on the Western Circuit and in 1888 was appointed one of the three senior Treasury Counsel. Twenty years later, in 1908, he was appointed Director of Public Prosecutions, an office he held until death.

His most famous case was when he appeared as Sir Edward Clarke's junior for Oscar Wilde in the private prosecution which he brought against the Marquis of Queensbery who was represented by Sir Edward Carson (q.v.).

He became the second President of the recently established Central Criminal Court Bar Mess when the title of that office was changed to Chairman and was thereafter to be held by the senior Treasury Counsel.

MR. CHARLES WILLIE MATHEWS

BORN in New York two-and-forty years ago, he found his way, while still a boy to Eton; and in spite of the lack of that manner and voice which are said to be more valuable at the Bar than legal wisdom, he determined to tempt Fate and juries. He was called twenty years ago, and, being quite open to histrionic influence as the step-son of Charles Mathews the Younger Celebrated Comedian, he naturally chose that branch of the profession in which the ability to assume (on behalf of a client) a virtue if he had it not is a possession of worth. His father's popularity with the play-going Bar of the last generation got him devilment under Mr. Montagu Williams, who was himself by way of being a theatrical person; and having thus gotten a start, he went on and made a criminal practice at the Old Bailey and on the Western Circuit; improving himself so much that, when Mr. Poland was called inside the Bar, he became Junior Prosecuting Counsel to the Treasury.

In Court he has a mincing manner that is full of affectation; yet out of Court he is an unaffected little fellow. He has also an unpleasantly high-pitched voice; but for this his pleasantly keen face makes amends, while his cool urbanity has been a marked success. He is not in great repute as a pleader, but he can marshal evidence; and, when they have grown used to his voice and manner, he can compel juries. He has been retained in some big cases.

He is full of youth; yet it is common report that he may be expected to look thirty by the end of the century.

"He can marshal evidence."

THOMAS ERSKINE MAY
(Baron Farnborough)

"PARLIAMENTARY PRACTICE"   **6th May 1871**

Parentage:
Born: 8th February 1815 in London.

Educated:
1826-1931 as a private pupil of Dr. Brereton, head-master of Bedford Grammar School.

Career:
Professional:
1831 - Assistant Librarian of the House of Commons.
1838 - Called to the Bar of the Middle Temple.
1844 - Published *A Practical Treatise on the Laws, Privileges, Proceedings and Usage of Parliament*, recognised by Parliament as authoritative and translated into German, French, Italian, Spanish, Japanese and Hungarian. The revised edition is still the standard work on the subject.
1847-1856 - Examiner of petitions for private bills and taxing master for both Houses.
1854 - Reduced into writing *Rules, Orders and Forms of Procedure of the House of Commons*, printed by order of the House.
1856-71 - Clerk-assistant.
1860 - C.B.
1866 - K.C.B.
1871 - Clerk of the House of Commons.
1873 - Bencher of the Middle Temple *Honoris Causa*.
1874 - D.C.L. (Oxon)
August 1885 - Sworn of the Privy Council.
April 1886 - Resigned.
May 1886 - Baron Farnborough of Farnborough in the County of Southampton.

Personal:
1830 - Married Louisa Johanna, only daughter of George Laughton of Fareham, Hants. No issue.

Died:
17th May 1886 at Westminster Palace. Public funeral service at St. Margaret's, Westminster, where a window was subsequently dedicated to his memory. Buried at Chippenham, Cambridge.

Since its first appearance in 1844, the work now known as *Erskine May's Parliamentary Practice* has been recognised as the bible of parliamentary procedure, not only in this country but also on the continent of Europe and throughout the British Commonwealth. No author enjoyed greater practical experience of his subject. He was a servant of the House of Commons for 55 years retiring only six months before his death. During the last 30 years he was in daily attendance in the Chamber itself and it was fitting that his death occurred in the Palace of Westminster.

It would be wrong to regard Erskine May as an *"homo unius libri"* as apart from his great work, and his digest of the rules of the House, *Rules, Orders and Forms of Procedure of the House of Commons* undertaken on the instructions of the House and published by its order, he also wrote *The Constitutional History of England Since The Accession of George III 1760-1860*, in effect a continuation of Hallam and *Democracy in Europe: A History*.

He was not indiscriminate in his praise of the forms of procedure of which his personal knowledge was so profound and published a pamphlet entitled *Remarks and Suggestions with a View to Facilitate the Despatch of Public Business in Parliament*, a bold action on the part of a civil servant.

SIR THOMAS ERSKINE MAY, K.C.B.

THE permanent Civil Service makes but small noise in the world and its members are scarcely ever known even by name to any but those who are directly engaged with them; nor do they, except in the rarest instances, ever gain a share in the honours and rewards that the State has to bestow. Nevertheless, it is they who carry on the heaviest and most important part of the business of the country, and who in all cases furnish the materials for the acts, and in many for the speeches of those who exclusively reap the honour and glory attached to public service. There are found among them many men of great ability and high attainments; but they are in general condemned to play a dumb part, and to sow in the dark the harvest that others reap.

Sir Erskine May is one of the few permanent public servants whose claims to honour are largely known and admitted. It is his rare distinction to have acquired fame, as well in the service of the State, as in literature. He has made a profound study of the constitutional system into which the modern ideas of popular Government have been cast, and has given the result of his researches to the world in works which have established his reputation as a Parliamentary jurist and historian. His official career has been passed in the House of Commons; and the history of that House, the phases through which its now stupendous power has passed, and the safeguards by which each successive addition to it has been surrounded, have engaged all his attention, so that he is now known as the first authority in all the mysteries of Parliamentary lore. As such he appropriately sits at the Table of the House of Commons as Clerk of the House, within easy and immediate reach of Mr. Speaker, with whom upon emergency he advises as "Chief of the Staff", and for whom he has more than once found an issue from a difficult position. He is the succour of the new and the refuge of the old member, and his ability is happily blended with so much tact and good-nature, that his authority is deferred to without hesitation and without jealousy.

"Parliamentary Practice"

CHARLES EDWARD POLLOCK

Parentage:

Born: 31st October 1823, fourth son of Sir Jonathan Frederick Pollock, Lord Chief Baron and 1st Bart. and his first wife, Frances, daughter of Francis Rivers. Brother of Major-General Sir Frederick Pollock and George Frederick Pollock, Queen's Remembrancer.

Educated:

St. Paul's School, London.

Career:

Professional:

1842 - Admitted Student at the Inner Temple.

1841 - 1844 - Secretary to his father when the latter was Attorney-General.

1846 - Marshall to his father upon his elevation to the Bench.

1847 - Called to the Bar of the Inner Temple.

"Tubman" and "Postman" of the Court of Exchequer.

July 1866 - Queen's Counsel.

November 1866 - Elected Bencher of the Inner Temple.

January 1873 - Baron of the Exchequer.

January 1873 - Invested with the coif.

February 1873 - Knighted.

Following the death of Baron Huddleston (5th December 1890) he became the last Baron of the Exchequer, and together with Lords Esher and Penzance and Sir Nathaniel (afterwards Lord) Lindley, he was one of the last Serjeants-at-Law. On the dissolution of Serjeant's Inn in 1882, he was re-elected Bencher of the Inner Temple. Wrote several law reports and text books.

General:

Member of the Commons Preservation Society. Chairman of the Conservators of Wimbledon Common.

Personal:

1848 - Married (1) Nicola Sophia second daughter of the Rev. Henry Herbert, Rector of Rathdowney, Queen's County, Ireland, (2) 1858 Georgiana, second daughter of George William Archibald, LL.D., Master of the Rolls in Nova Scotia. (3) 1865 Amy Henella, daughter of Hassard Hume Dodgson, Master of the Court of Common Pleas, second cousin of Charles Lutwidge Dodgson (Lewis Carroll), by all of whom he had issue.

Died:

21st November 1897 at The Croft, Putney.

Charles Pollock, like so many judges of his time, came from a distinguished legal family. He was better known at the Bar as an author than as an advocate and wrote a number of reports and works on practice.

He was the last Baron of the Exchequer. After 1873 all High Court Judges were styled "Mr. Justice —" but the existing Judges retained their title. He was one of the last Serjeants-at-law; the Serjeants had been the highest rank of barrister and enjoyed the exclusive right of audience in the Court of Common Pleas. Only Serjeants could be appointed Judges and if not already Serjeants were invested with the coif on appointment. With the Judicature Act of 1873 no new Serjeants were appointed.

He tried the famous case of R. v. Keyn [Cox CC XIII 403]. Kyne, the Master of the German steamship "Franconia", was tried for manslaughter following a collision with the "Strathclyde" within three miles of the English coast. Keyn was convicted but Pollock reserved the question of jurisdiction to the Court of Crown Cases Reserved and was one of the majority there that quashed the conviction.

He was much interested in preserving commons and open spaces and was a Conservator of Wimbledon Common. It was largely due to his efforts that this remained an open space on the outskirts of London.

THE HON. SIR CHARLES EDWARD POLLOCK

THE POLLOCKS are a large family, and most of its members having shown that they know how to take care of themselves, they are supposed to be a clever family also. Two generations ago, one David came from Scotland to Piccadilly, where selling his wares to the Southron he accumulated much money and many children; of whom two were sent to law, with the result that one became a Chief Justice in Bombay, and another a Chief Baron of the Exchequer. To this Chief Baron was born some score of young Pollocks, who are known by their severely legal faces and by their legal and other successes. Born seven-and-sixty years ago, his fourth son, Charles Edward, was sent to school with Sir James Hannen and the late Serjeant Ballantine, just in time to become his father's Private Secretary when the late Chief Baron became Attorney-General; after which he naturally went to the Bar with such considerable advantages that, after some briefless years passed in book-writing, he achieved a Judgeship seventeen years ago, being made the last Baron but one of the Court of Exchequer in 1873.

There is nothing remarkable in his legal history; but he is known for his unfailing courtesy, his quiet dignity, and his dispassionate trial of cases. No Judge shows himself more anxious to settle the cases that come before him. He is a kindly man, even to criminals; and he never loses his temper. Yet it is said of him and of Mr. Justice Denman by irreverent juniors that they are Judges *per stirpes* and not *per capita*.

He has done what he might to perpetuate his honoured name by marrying three times. He is a good man and a Conservative, who is as much respected in Putney, where he lives, as he is in Court; and he has sometimes honoured a local political meeting with much grace and dignity.

He is not so good a lawyer as he looks.

"One of the Family"

CHARLES RUSSELL
(Lord Russell of Killowen)

"A SPLENDID ADVOCATE"   **5th May 1883**

Parentage:
Born: 10th November 1832 at Newry, eldest son of Arthur Russell (1785 - 1845) and Margaret, daughter of Matthew Mullin and widow of John Hamill of Belfast, merchant.

Educated:
Diocesan Seminary, Belfast, two years at a private school in Newry and one year at St. Vincent's College, Castleknock.

Career:
Professional:
1849 - Articled to Cornelius Denvir, solicitor of Newry.
1852 - On the latter's death, articles transferred to Alexander O'Rorke of Belfast.
1854 - Admitted as solicitor.
1856 - Entered Lincoln's Inn.
1859 - Called to the Bar of Lincoln's Inn.
1872 - Queen's Counsel.
1886 - 1887 - Attorney-General
1892 - Attorney-General
1892 - G.C.M.G.
May 1894 - Lord Justice of Appeal and created a Life Peer as Lord Russell of Killowen.
June 1894 - Lord Chief Justice of England.

Political:
1880 - Returned for Dundalk after two unsuccessful attempts as an independent Liberal.
1885 - Returned for South Hackney which he represented until his elevation to the Bench.

Personal:
1858 - Married Ellen, eldest daughter of Joseph Stevenson Mulholland, M.D. of Belfast. Five sons and Four daughters.

Died:
10th August 1900 at 2 Cromwell Houses, Kensington. Buried at Epsom.

Charles Russell came from an ancient Catholic family living in County Down. He started his career as a solicitor and made his name defending Catholics involved in the anti-Protestant riots of 1855. The speeches were reported in *The Ulsterman* and he was carried shoulder high to his hotel.

He moved to London and read for the Bar, paying for his living expenses by becoming a successful journalist and contributor to the Dublin *Nation*.

As soon as he qualified as a barrister his rise was meteoric and he became famous for his skill at cross-examination. His maxim was: "Go straight at the witness and at the point; throw your cards on the table; mere finesse English juries do not appreciate".

His greatest triumph was his defence of Charles Parnell and 65 Irish Members of Parliament before the Parnell Commission, established to investigate allegations in *The Times* that they were in collusion with Fenian terrorists. As a result of his cross-examination over two days Richard Pigott, the principal witness against Parnell, fled the country and wrote from Paris admitting his forgery of the incriminating letters. During the hearing someone asked Sir James Hannan, the presiding Judge, how Russell was doing: "Master Charlie is bowling very straight" was the reply.

MR. CHARLES RUSSELL, Q.C., M.P.

MR. RUSSELL was born in Newry fifty years ago. Like most able men, he owes much to the early training of a singularly good mother. She gave him an excellent education, and in deference to her wishes he adopted the profession of a solicitor in Belfast; but conscious of greater powers than could thus find scope for their exercise, he soon transferred himself to the Bar, to which he was called at the age of six-and-twenty. Coming to England with excellent letters of recommendation, he at once achieved success in the Court of Passage at Liverpool, where he rapidly acquired a very lucrative practice. But it is in London that his great career has been made. He distinguished himself in the great case of Saurin v. Starr, as junior counsel to Lord (then Sir John) Coleridge, and in a marvellously short time made it apparent that in him a new legal luminary had arisen. In 1872 he was made a Queen's Counsel, in 1874 he became Member of Parliament for Dundalk, a town which he had previously twice contested without success, and he is now indisputably the foremost advocate at the English Bar.

Mr. Russell is a man of extraordinary abilities. He has all the brilliant qualities and discloses none of the countervailing defects that we are accustomed to recognise in the very best kind of Irishman. Industrious and capable of long-sustained work when industry affords the only possible means of mastering the matter in hand, he is yet more remarkable still for the unerring precision and instant certainty with which he flies through the mass of surrounding circumstances at the truly vital point of a case. His judgment has rarely yet been found at fault, and when he appears in Court he is a marvel. His clear and resonant voice; his grand and impassive presence; his commanding power over men, whether they be enthroned on the bench, seated among the jury, or pilloried in the witness-box; the lucidity and energy of his exposition; and the conclusive point and vigour of his argument, are such as, taken together, make him appear rather as a giant among pigmies than as a competitor among equals. Therewith he has a tenacity of purpose, a firmness and an unflinching courage which make him personally a no less redoubtable antagonist than he is a splendid advocate, and few men have tried a fall with him who have not arisen from it seriously damaged.

Mr. Russell is a man of various tastes and acquirements, which he cultivates in spite of an enormous mass of business. While yet a boy he learned to love the sea; he is an excellent judge of a horse and a snuff; he is a good whip; he occasionally trifles, during his rare intervals of leisure, with horse-racing and whist; and he is besides a personage of much importance in the House of Commons, where his speeches are always listened to with great attention and respect. Withal he is a man who, however terrible of aspect to the adversary, is found a most rare and brilliant companion by his friends.

"a splendid advocate"

THOMAS EDWARD SCRUTTON

"COPYRIGHT"   **28th June 1911**

Parentage:
Born: 28th August 1856 in East India Dock Road, Poplar, eldest son of Thomas Urquhart Scrutton, a prosperous ship-owner, late of Buckhurst Hill, Essex and of Mary, daughter of the Rev. Edward Hickman. His father's family had for several generations run a line of vessels, originally under sail between the U.K. and the West Indies.

Educated:
Mill Hill School and London University. Graduated B.A. proceeded M.A. and 1882 LL.B., all with Honours. Scholar of Trinity College, Cambridge. 1879 First Class in the Moral Sciences Tripos and Senior Whewell Scholar for International Law. 1880 First in the First Class of the Law Tripos. 1882, 1884, 1885, 1886 Yorke Prizeman (Legal Essay).

Career:
Professional:
1882 - Barstow Scholarship of the Inns of Court.
1882 - Called to the Bar of the Middle Temple.
1901 - Queen's Counsel.
1908 - Elected Bencher of the Middle Temple.
1910 - Appointed a Judge of the King's Bench Division of the High Court of Justice. He often sat in the Commercial Court. Knighted.
1916 - Raised to the Court of Appeal and sworn of the Privy Council. Died in office. Author of *Scrutton on Charter Parties*.

Political:
1886 - Contested Limehouse in the Liberal interest.

General:
Presented the Scrutton Cup for an annual golf competition between the Inns of Court.

Personal:
1884 - Married Mary, daughter of Samuel Crickmer Burton, solicitor of Great Yarmouth. Had issue four sons and a daughter.

Died:
18 November, 1934 at Norwich.

Thomas Scrutton came from a long-established family of ship-owners who were staunch Congregationalists. It is therefore fitting that he should be best remembered for his monumental work *The Contract of Affreightment as expressed in Charterparties and Bills of Lading*, better known as *Scrutton on Charter Parties*. Scrutton himself was, at the end of life, monumental - tall and very stoutly built.

Despite a distinguished career at the Universities of London and Cambridge, he failed to obtain a fellowship at Trinity and shortly after his death Sir J.J. Thomson remarked of him: "I remember Scrutton. A very clever man of immense industry but - no originality."

In 1915 he tried the notorious case of R. v. George Joseph Smith [11 Cr. App. Rep. 229] at The Old Bailey. Smith was tried for the murder of Bessie Munday with whom he had gone through a form of marriage and whom he claimed he had found drowned in her bath. It was Scrutton's decision to admit evidence of the deaths of two other ladies, Alice Burnham and Margaret Lofty in precisely similar circumstances under the Rule in Makin v. Att. Gen. for New South Wales [(1894) AC 57] which secured his conviction and led to the press dubbing the case "The Brides in the Bath Murders".

He sat on appeal on the "Helen of Troy" case, Place v. Searle [(1932) 2 K.B.497] on appeal from the judgment of McCardie, J., an action for enticing the Plaintiff's wife which McCardie, J. had withdrawn from the jury. Scrutton made such scathing remarks about McCardie's judgment that in the next appeal McCardie refused to send his notes if Scrutton was to sit.

MR. JUSTICE SCRUTTON

ALERT, incisive, the very personification of dignified solidity, the Hon. Sir T. Edward Scrutton - apart from his exalted position as one of the judges of his Majesty's King's Bench Division - is, in many ways, a remarkable personage. He is almost appallingly learned in the law and in the tortuosities of its application to commercial life. What he does not know about copyright is not worth knowing, and as to shipping law he is a walking encyclopaedia.

His scholastic career was a record of continuous successes, exemplifying to the full the value of persistency in intelligent painstaking.

The son of Mr. Thomas Scrutton, shipowner, of Buckhurst Hill, Essex, Mr. Justice Scrutton was born on August 28th 1856, and first went to Mill Hill School. Thence he proceeded to University College, London (of which he eventually became a Fellow), and completed his academic course at Cambridge University.

At Trinity College, Cambridge, he was a Foundation Scholar. He captured the coveted Senior Whewell Scholarship at the University. His educational achievements make a lengthy list. First Class Moral Science Tripos, 1879, and Senior Law Tripos, 1880 are prominent amongst them. Four times he carried off the Yorke Prize. The University of London gave him his M.A. degree and in the competition for this he obtained marks qualifying for the medal. In gaining his B.A. he took First Class Honours in English, and Honours in Classics and Moral Science; and he got the LL.B. with First Class Honours in Roman Law and Jurisprudence.

Devoting himself thenceforth to the law, he went to the Inns of Court as Barstow Scholar in 1882, and he was a scholar of the Middle Temple. Thence he received his call to the Bar, and ultimately he was elected a Bencher of his Inn.

As a barrister he acquired a large practice in commercial cases, and engaged assiduously at the same time in literary labours in connection with the legal subjects to which he was devoting particular attention. His "Treatise on the Law of Copyright" is as authoritative as it is monumental, and so much in request was it that it quickly passed through four editions This was given first to the world in 1883; and three years thereafter he published his "Law of Charter Parties and Bills of Lading", now in its sixth edition. In 1894 this was followed by another erudite work on the Merchant Shipping Act, also in great demand in legal and commercial circles.

Mr. Scrutton was made a K.C. in 1901, and preferred to a judgeship of the King's Bench Division of the High Court in 1910. Meantime he had acted as counsel to important newspapers, and acquired a position almost unique in matters of copyright, reference, and the like.

Married in 1884 to Mary, daughter of Mr. S.C. Burton, J.P., of Great Yarmouth, he resides at Westcombe Park, and there, in the intervals of his strenuous professional life, has entertained lavishly - for his circle of friends is large. In 1886 he contested the Limehouse Division of the Tower Hamlets in the Liberal interest, but was not successful in this his one attempt to enter the House of Commons. He belongs still to the Reform Club, and is a familiar figure at the Athenaeum.

His amazing profundity is no bar to the perennial flow of good humour which characterises him as a man.

"Copyright."

BARON SHAND
(Alexander Burns Shand)

Parentage:
Born: 13th December 1828 at Aberdeen, son of Alexander Shand, merchant in Aberdeen and Louisa, daughter of John Whyte, M.D. of Banff. His grandfather, John Shand, was parish minister of Kintore. Following his father's death his mother married William Burns, Writer of Glasgow, whose surname he took.

Educated:
1842 - 1848 - Glasgow University, whilst also working in his stepfather's office. 1848 - 1852 - Law student at Edinburgh University and a short time at Heidelburg University.

Career:
Professional:
1852 - Member of the Scots Law Society and of the Juridical Society.
1853 - Passed to the Scottish Bar.
1860 - Advocate-Depute.
1862 - Sheriff of Kincardine.
1869 - Sheriff of Haddington and Berwick.
1872 - Raised to the Bench.
1890 - Retired and settled in London.
November 1890 - Took his seat at the Board of the Judicial Committee.
March 1892 - Elected an Honorary Bencher of Gray's Inn.
August 1892 - Created Baron Shand of Woodhouse, Dumfriesshire. Sat as a Lord of Appeal in the House of Lords. Died in office.

General:
President of the Watt Institute and School of Arts in Edinburgh.
1882 - Member of the Educational Endowments Commission.
1894 - Chairman of the Coal Industry Conciliation Board.
1873 - Honorary LL.D. (Glasgow).
1895 - Honorary D.C.L. (Oxon).

Personal:
1857 - Married Emily Merelina (d.1911) daughter of John Clarke Meymott. No issue.

Died:
6th March 1904 at London. Buried at Kintore in Aberdeenshire.

Alexander Shand began his legal career in the offices of his stepfather, William Burns, a Writer in Glasgow, the Scottish equivalent of a solicitor. Thoroughly and widely educated at Glasgow, Edinburgh and for a time Heidelburg Universities his career in the law was distinguished and his rise rapid.

Since the Act of Union of 1701, the House of Lords, sitting in London, had been the final Court of Appeal for civil cases from Scotland. However, until the last quarter of the 19th Century, no steps were taken to ensure a supply of Scottish Law Lords to hear such cases. The appointment of such Judges as Shand, Gordon (q.v.) and Lord Colonsay (q.v.) did much to remedy this defect and not only Scottish but also English law was the gainer.

The most memorable case on which he sat was a dispute between the dissenting minority "The Wee Frees" and The Free Prestbyterian Church, following the latter's union with the United Prestbyterians. The "Wee Frees" claimed the whole of the Free Church's property. The claim was heard by six Law Lords and finished on 7th December, 1903. Shand and two others are believed to have upheld the judgment of the Court of Session dismissing the claim and in the event of a tie the judgment below would have been upheld. However he died on 6th March 1904 before the reserved judgment could be delivered and the case was re-heard by seven Law Lords who upheld the claim of the "Wee Frees" provoking the comment that "the dead hand came down with a resounding slap on the living body".

THE BARON SHAND

ALEXANDER BURNS SHAND, P.C., D.C.L., LL.D., son of Alexander Shand of Aberdeen, is five-and-seventy years old, the holder of a Peerage created eleven years ago, a vara wee man, and vara Scotch. His education was varied, for it was achieved at Glasgow, Edinburgh and Heidelberg; yet he still talks Scotch. He is an Honorary Graduate of Oxford University, an Honorary Bencher of Gray's Inn, and a member of the Athenaeum Club; while he has been Sheriff of Kincardineshire, of Haddington, and of Berwick; a Judge of the Court of Session (where one learns real wit); a Deputy-Lieutenant of Edinburgh City; a Commissioner under the Educational Endowments Act for Scotland, and many other wholesome Scottish things: besides which he was well nominated Chairman of the Coal Industry Conciliation Board some nine years ago. Scots Law is popularly believed to be a thing which only a great intellect can master; but Lord Shand has mastered as much of that erudition as any one man has ever been known to master. That is why he was promoted from the Scottish Bench to be a supernumerary Law Lord; and his promotion was received by the profession with general approval. And so, having all his life through been devoted to golf, he now plays the game in company with the Lord Chancellor or the Speaker; and he has even been known to play with the Prime Minister. Although he is not a long driver, he is so beloved of golfers that on one well-known links a bunker is named after him simply because he has been seen in it so often.

Nevertheless, his wee body supports a head that is chock full of legal lore tempered by much acumen.

"a Scots lawyer"

ARCHIBALD LEVIN SMITH

Parentage:
Born: 27th August 1836 at Salt Hill, Chichester, Sussex only son of Francis Smith and Mary Ann, only daughter of Zadik Levin.

Educated:
Eton and Trinity College, Cambridge where he graduated B.A. in 1858.

Career:
Professional:
1856 - Entered the Inner Temple.
1860 - Called to the Bar of the Inner Temple.
1879 - Standing Junior Counsel to the Treasury.
1883 - Appointed a Judge of the Queen's Bench Division of the High Court of Justice.
1883 - Elected Bencher of the Inner Temple.
April 1883 - Knighted.
1888 - Appointed a Special Commissioner with Sir James Hannan and Day, J. to enquire into allegations published in *The Times* affecting C.S. Parnell and other Irish nationalists.
1892 - Lord Justice of Appeal.
October 1900 - Master of the Rolls.

General:
1857, 1858 and 1859 - Rowed in the inter-university boat race. On the last occasion the Cambridge boat filled and sunk between Barnes Bridge and the finish. Played cricket for the Gentlemen of Sussex, 1899 President of the Marylebone Cricket Club.

Personal:
1867 - Married Isobel, daughter of John Charles Fletcher. Two sons and three daughters.

Died:
20th October 1901 at Wester-Elchies House, Aberlour, Morayshire, the residence of his son-in-law, Mr. Grant and buried at Knockando, Morayshire. His wife, after a long and distressing illness, was drowned in the Spey near Aberlour in the preceding August almost in his presence. He resigned his office a few days before his death.

Archibald Smith hailed from a Sussex family, was educated at Eton and Cambridge and like Sir Joseph Chitty (q.v.) was a good oarsman at both school and University. He rowed in three consecutive boat races although in the last one his boat sunk and as he could not swim there were problems getting him to the shore.

He built up a good junior practice mainly in commercial cases and election petitions. Somewhat unusually he was appointed to the Bench straight from the Junior Bar, having been Standing Junior Counsel to the Treasury for only four years.

With Sir James Hannan and Day, J. he was one of the three commissioners appointed under the Parnell Commission Act 1888 to enquire into the allegations made in *The Times* against Charles Parnell and 65 Members of the Irish Parliament accusing them of complicity in Fenian violence. Parnell and his colleagues were represented by Sir Charles Russell (q.v.). On one occasion the President, Hannan, said that he had not thought or imputed something of which some of those appearing before the Commission had complained. "Nor I", said Smith, the only words he uttered during the length of proceedings. Day merely grunted and that was the sum total of his contribution.

THE HON. SIR ARCHIBALD LEVIN SMITH

HE is the son of the late Francis Smith, Esq., J.P., of Salt Hill, Chichester, whose wife was a Miss Levin of the same place; and he perpetuates the names of both his parents. Born in 1836, educated at Eton and Trinity, Cambridge, he was called to the Bar eight-and-twenty years ago, when he commenced the successful career which has lately culminated in his appointment as Third Commissioner to inquire into the journalistic Charges and Allegations the truth of which is now being so tediously investigated in Probate Court I. of the Royal Courts of Justice. His education failed to make either a prig or a great scholar of him; but his legal experience and sound common sense have since combined to make him a Judge who has no superior amongst his puisne brethren. His rise has been as rapid as it was deserved; for he showed enough practical sense in his conduct of such cases as fell into his hands early in his career to impress Lord Justice Bowen, then Attorney-General's "devil," with his quality, and, as a consequence, he became himself an imp of less degree, being appointed the devil's devil. That was all that was necessary to make the man, and when his master soared up to the Bench, Mr. Smith became a full-blown devil, in which capacity he counselled the Treasury so wisely that five years ago he was rewarded by being promoted to the position which he now occupies over the heads of all the Queen's Counsel of the day.

He is not a very brilliant man, but his mental grasp is most comprehensive. He drinks in a new Act of Parliament while other men skim its first section, and intricate accounts in a big commercial case are a delightful exercise to his well-trained mind. He is very lucid, very popular, very good-natured, and very free from serious fault. He never acts, never wastes time, and never sermonises even to criminals when they are found guilty before him. He does not respect persons, he does not advertise, nor does he shirk the most unpleasant work. All which is high praise, but merited both by what he does and what he does not. Not having the gift of tongue in any marked degree, his charges to juries are choppy, and occasionally monotonous; but, being brief, clear, and always to the point, they are none the worse for that. There is only one more youthful Judge on the Bench; but there is also, take him for all in all, only one better. Being wealthy, he works rather for the good of others than himself; and having never been corrupted by Parliament, or by any other form of politics, he is extremely well adapted for the temporary office which he now occupies. He is always courteous even to the more foolish, and consequently more irritating, among juniors. He has much high spirit and much muscular strength; and his shoulders are types of the tremendous, with which he did stout service in the Cambridge Eight. He still loves exercise and the fresh air of Sussex. He is a jolly good fellow, who looks more like a sturdy English Squire than like the good Judge that he is. He is well favoured in all senses and he wears a pair of *pince-nez* at the end of his nose.

"3rd Commissioner"

FREDERICK EDWIN SMITH
(Earl of Birkenhead)

"NO SURRENDER"   **9th August 1911**

Parentage:
Born: 12th July 1872 at Birkenhead, eldest son of Frederick Smith, Estate Agent, Barrister of the Middle Temple and sometime Mayor of Birkenhead (d. 1887) and Elizabeth, daughter of Edwin Taylor of Birkenhead.

Educated:
Birkenhead School and Open Classic Scholar, Wadham College, Oxford (1893). Second Class in Mods (1895). First in Jurisprudence (1896). Elected Vinerian scholar and fellow of Merton College and law tutor (1897). Law tutor at Oriel College, Oxford.

Career:
Professional:
1894 - Entered Gray's Inn.
1899 - Called to the Bar of Gray's Inn.
1908 - Queen's Counsel.
May 1915 - Solicitor-General.
November 1915 - Attorney-General.
1917 - Treasurer of Gray's Inn.
1918 - Created a Baronet.
January 1919 - Received the Great Seal.
February 1919 - Created Baron Birkenhead.
June 1921 - Created Viscount Furneaux.
October 1922 - Resigned with the Ministry. Created Earl of Birkenhead and Viscount Furneaux D.C.L. and High Steward of Oxford.
October 1924 - Secretary of State for India.
1928 - Resigned. Created G.C.S.I.

Political:
1906 - M.P. for the Walton Division of Liverpool.
1918 - M.P. for the West Derby Division of Liverpool.

Personal:
1901 - Married Margaret Eleanor, second daughter of the Rev. Henry Furneaux, fellow of Corpus Christi College, Oxon, the editor of Tacitus. Had one son, Frederick Winston Furneaux (b.1907), 2nd Earl, and two daughters.

Died:
30th September 1930 at London.

"F.E." came from a well-established Liverpudlian family and his father was the distinguished Conservative Mayor of Birkenhead, which helped greatly with F.E.'s political career. He was one of the most brilliant men of his generation, being appointed Lord Chancellor at the remarkably early age of 47.

He first entered Parliament in 1906 for the Walton Division of Liverpool. Politics in Liverpool were then dominated by the Irish question and Smith was always a staunch Loyalist. There is no doubt that he was involved in the smuggling of arms into Ulster for Carson's Ulster Volunteers.

As a lawyer he made his name in the case brought by William Lever, M.P., afterwards Lord Leverhulme, of the soap manufacturers Lever Brothers, against Lord Northcliffe's newspapers, notably *The Daily Mail*, which was settled for agreed damages of £50,000. His defence of Ethel le Neve, Crippens' mistress, in which he secured her acquittal on a charge of being accessory to murder, brought his name before a wider public.

He is now best remembered for the new property legislation which he steered through a largely indifferent Parliament in 1925, including the Law of Property Act, the Land Registration Act, the Settled Land Act, the Trustee Act and the Administration of Estates Act which transformed the English Law of Real Property and Succession.

FREDERICK EDWIN SMITH, M.P., K.C., M.A., B.C.L.

S INCE the Tory Party entered the cool shades of opposition Mr. F.E. Smith, the rising barrister and energetic politician, has loomed largely in the political horizon. His career down to the present time has been brilliant and meteoric, but his precise position in the party is not yet clearly defined. Perhaps his action in connection with the final stages of the struggle between the Government and the House of Lords may interfere for a time with his prospects, but that there will be a reshuffling of the political cards there can be no doubt.

One thing seems tolerably certain, that the main Conservative Party, whatever may be its ultimate constitution, can scarcely afford to dispense with the services of so good a speaker and so able a lawyer. Some lawyers have in the past deliberately selected the Tory political platform as the sphere of operations because of the greater scope and limited competition as compared with the profession of Liberal opinions.

On the platform he evokes the utmost sympathy and enthusiasm from his audience, but in the House of Commons itself he has been a tower of strength to his party. His Law Courts speeches and manner are a bit disappointing to his political admirers who may happen to come in contact with him in that connection, but after all "nothing succeeds like success," and Mr. Smith enjoys a reputation as an advocate of the front rank, and his briefs are always most generously marked.

It was no error of judgement, but really a fine tactical move, when Mr. F.E. Smith was introduced as Parliamentary candidate to the electors of the Scotland Division of Liverpool in opposition to Mr. T.P. O'Connor. He did not win his seat, but made a useful reputation and, of course, was wanted for the Walton Division.

Mr. Smith was born at Birkenhead in 1872, so that he has ample time to pull himself together, and if he continues with the astuteness that has distinguished all his movements his "arrival" with the new order of Conservatism is only a question of time.

In some quarters Mr. Smith is regarded as a bitter and even a vitriolic partisan, but those who know him intimately declare him to be a most kindly and genial personality, without a spice of malice in his nature.

The anomalies and strenuousness of political life lead to such misconception. Mr. Smith also is suspected of being on the most cordial and friendly terms with Mr. Winston Churchill, and it is doubtful which of the two suffers most in public estimation by the association.

We may look forward to hearing more of this young man in a hurry in the near future. Office appears a long way off, and things are not moving fast enough in his party to suit him.

Mr. Smith is of a simple and retiring disposition. His favourite pastimes are "Battledore-and-Shuttlecock" and "Follow-my-Leader". He used to read *The Daily Mail*.

"No Surrender."

Table of Cases

Bradford Corporation v. Pickles (1805) A.C. 587 - see Cozens-Hardy

McNaughten's case (1843) 10 Cl. & Fin. 200 - see Cockburn

Makin v. Att. Gen. for New South Wales (1894) A.C. 57 - see Scrutton

Place v. Searle (1932) 2.K.B. 497 - see Scrutton

R. v. Casement (1917) 1 K.B. 98 - see Isaacs/Darling

R. v. Castro (or Orton) (1874) L.R. 9 Q.B. - 350 - see Cockburn

R. v. Frost 4 St. Tr. (N.S.) 85 - see Kelly

R. v. Keyn Cox C.C. XIII, 403 - see Pollock

R. v. Mylius (Times, Feb. 2, 1911) - see Isaacs

R. v. Newman (1853) IE & B 558 - see Kelly

R. v. Smith 11, Cr. App.Rep. 229 - see Scrutton

Walsh & Lonsdale (1882) 21 Ch. D. 9 - see Jessel

Yelverton v. Longworth (1864) 10 Jur. N.S. 1209 H.L. - see Gordon

Some Nom de Crayons of
Vanity Fair Artists

APE .... CARLO PELLEGRINI (1839 - 1899)

APE JUNIOR .... ROLAND L'ESTRANGE (1869 - 1919)

COIDE .... J. J. TISSOT (1836 - 1902)

FCG .... SIR FRANCIS CARRUTHERS GOULD (1844 - 1925)

FTD .... F.T. DALTON (active Vanity Fair 1894 - 1900)

GDG .... GODFREY GILES (1857 - 1923)

GUTH .... JEAN BAPTISTE GUTH (active Vanity Fair 1889 - 1910)

LIB .... LIBERIO PROSPERI (active Vanity Fair 1885 - 1903)

QUIZ .... J. P. MELLOR (active Vanity Fair 1889 - 1899)

SIC .... W. R. SICKERT (1860 - 1942)

SINGE .... Early Italian pseudonym for APE

SPY .... SIR LESLIE WARD (1851 - 1922)

STUFF .... H. C. WRIGHT (1850 - 1937)

T .... THO CARTRAN (1849 - 1907)

WV .... Unconfirmed, but perhaps W. Vine

Appendix A

SUBJECT	CAPTION	YEAR	ARTIST
A			
Alverstone, Lord	Dick	1900	SPY
Alverstone, Lord	Lord Chief Justice	1913	WH
Askwith, Sir George R., K.C.	The Conciliator	1911	WH
Asquith, Mr. Herbert Henry	East Fife	1891	SPY
Asquith, The Rt. Hon. Herbert Henry M.P.	Brains	1904	SPY
Asquith, The Rt. Hon. Herbert Henry K.C., M.P.	A Great Orator	1910	XIT
Avory, Mr. Horace, K.C.	Slim	1904	SPY
B			
Bacon, His Honour Judge	A Judicial Joker	1897	SPY
Bacon, The Hon. Sir James,	Contempt of Court	1873	VW
Baggallay, Mr. Ernest	A Popular Magistrate	1905	SPY
Baggallay, Sir Richard	The Court of Appeals	1875	APE
Balfour, The Rt. Hon. John Blair, P.C., M.P.	The Lord Advocate	1886	SPY
Ballantine, Serjeant	He Resisted Temptation	1870	UNSIGNED
Bankes, John Eldon, K.C.	Good Form	1906	SPY
Barnes, The Hon. Sir John Gorell	Admiralty Jurisdiction	1893	SPY
Barry, Lord Justice	Lord Justice Barry	1889	LIB
Barton, Mr. Dunbar Plunket, Q.C., M.P.	Mid Armagh	1898	SPY
Barton, Sir Edmund P.C., K.C.	Australia	1902	SPY
Beard, Mr. Thomas	Under Sheriff	1891	SPY
Beaurepaire, M. Quesnay De	As Procureur General	1893	GUTH
Belilios, Mr. R.E.	Billy	1910	PIP
Bhownaggree, Sir Merwanjee, K.C.I.E., M.P.	Northeast Bethnal Green	1897	SPY
Bigham, Mr. Justice	We Shall See	1898	SPY
Biron, Mr. H.C.	Worship Street	1907	SPY
Blackburn, Lord	A Lord of Appeal	1881	SPY
Bosanquet, Mr. Frederick Albert K.C.	Bosey, Frederick	1901	SPY
Bovill, Chief Justice	The Majesty of the Law	1870	APE
Bowen, The Rt. Hon. Sir Charles Synge Christopher	Judicial Politeness	1892	SPY
Bowyer, Sir George, Bart., M.P.	The Knight of Malta	1879	SPY
Bramwell, Sir Frederick Joseph, Bart.	An Arbitrator	1892	SPY
Bramwell, The Hon. Sir George William Wilshere	The Exchequer	1876	SPY
Bray, Mr. Justice	A Man of Law and Broad Acres	1906	SPY
Brett, Sir William Baliol	Popular Judgment	1876	APE
Bright, John, & Group	Birth, Behaviour & Business	1881	T
Brisson, M. Henri	Justice to Dreyfus	1898	GUTH
Broadley, Mr. Alexander Meyrick	He Defended Arabi	1889	SPY
Bruce, Mr. Gainsford	Holborn	1892	SPY
Bruce, Mr. Justice	Slow and Steady	1900	SPY
Buckley, Mr. Justice	Company Law	1900	SPY
Buckmaster, Stanley	The Solicitor-General	1913	OWL
Bucknill, Mr. Justice	Tommy	1900	SPY
Butcher, Mr. John George, K.C.	York City	1901	SPY
Butt, Sir Charles Parker	Divorce	1887	APE
Byrne, Mr. Edmund Widdrington, Q.C., M.P.	Chitty's Leader	1896	SPY
C			
Carden, Alderman Sir Robert, KT., M.P.	City Justice	1880	SPY
Carson, Mr. E.H.	Dublin University	1893	LIB
Carson, Sir Edward H. K.T., K.C., M.P.	Dublin University	1911	HESTER
Carson, The Rt. Hon. Sir Edward P.C., K.T., K.C., M.P.	I Never Ask Anyone	1912	WH

SUBJECT	CAPTION	YEAR	ARTIST
Cave, The Hon. Sir L.W.	That Won't Do, You Know	1893	SPY
Cecil, Lord Robert, K.C., M.P.	So Voluble An Advocate	1906	SPY
Chambers, Sir Thomas, Q.C, M.P.	The Deceased Wife's Sister	1884	SPY
Channell, Mr. Justice	An Amiable Judge	1898	SPY
Charles, The Rt. Hon. Sir Arthur	The New Judge	1888	SPY
Chitty, The Hon. Sir Joseph William	The Umpire	1885	SPY
Clarke, Sir Edward George, K.C.	Sir Edward	1903	SPY
Cleasby, The Hon. Sir Anthony	Formerly of the Carlton	1876	SPY
Cock, Mr. Alfred	He Has Leathern Lungs	1891	STUFF
Cockburn, Rt. Hon. Sir Alexander, J.E., Bart.	The Lord Chief Justice	1869	APE
Coleridge, Lord	The Silvered Voice	1909	SPY
Coleridge, Lord	The Lord Chief Justice	1887	APE
Coleridge, Sir John D.	A Risen Barrister	1870	ATN
Collier, Sir Robert P.	Sir John Coleridge	1870	UNSIGNED
Collins, The Hon. Sir R.H.	Smith's Leading Case	1893	QUIZ
Colonsay, Lord	Scotch Law	1873	SPY
Cotton, The Rt. Hon. Lord Justice	Guileless	1888	SPY
Cozens-Hardy, Mr. H., Q.C.	North Norfolk	1893	SPY
Cozens-Hardy, The Hon. Mr.Justice	Fair, if not Beautiful	1901	SPY
Cripps, Mr. Charles Alfred, D.C.	Vicar General	1902	SPY
Curzon, Viscount, M.P.	South Bucks	1896	SPY

D

SUBJECT	CAPTION	YEAR	ARTIST
Danckwerts, Mr.	Danky	1898	SPY
Darling, Mr. Charles John, Q.C., M.P.	Little Darling	1897	SPY
Darling, Mr. Justice	Judicial Light Weight	1907	SPY
Day, The Hon. Sir John Frederick Sigismund Charles	2nd Commissioner	1888	SPY
Deane, Mr. Henry Bargrave Finnelly, Q.C.	Bargrave	1898	SPY
Denison, Mr. Speaker	The First of the Commoners	1870	ATN
Denman, The Hon. George	He Was an Ornament	1892	STUFF
Desart, The Earl Of	Public Prosecutions	1902	SPY
Dickens, Mr. Henry Fielding, Q.C.	His Father Invented Pickwick	1897	SPY
Dowse, Mr. Richard M.P.	An Irish Wit	1871	APE

E

SUBJECT	CAPTION	YEAR	ARTIST
Eady, The Hon. Mr. Justice Swinfen,	Plausible	1902	SPY
Edlin, Sir Peter Henry	London Sessions	1891	SPY
Ellenborough, The Lord	Law	1886	SPY
Elliott, Mr. George	George	1908	SPY
Elton, Mr. Charles Isaac, Q.C., M.P.	Court Roll	1887	SPY
Eve, Mr. Justice	A Good Judge	1911	APE JR

F

SUBJECT	CAPTION	YEAR	ARTIST
Farwell, Mr. Justice	Powers	1900	FTD
Field, Mr. Justice	Stay Please	1887	SPY
Finlay, Mr. Robert Bannatyne, Q.C., M.D., M.P.	Hard Head	1888	APE
Fordham, Mr. Edward Snow	North London	1908	SPY
Fry, The Rt. Hon. Sir Edward	Specific Performance	1891	SPY
Fulton, Sir Forest, The Recorder of London.	The Recorder	1903	SPY

G

SUBJECT	CAPTION	YEAR	ARTIST
Gibson, The Rt. Hon. Edward, P.C., Q.C., LL.D.	Dublin University	1885	SPY
Giffard, Sir Hardinge Stanley	The Solicitor-General	1878	SPY
Gill, Mr. Charles Frederick	Gill Brass	1891	SPY
Goldsmid, Sir Francis Henry, Bart., M.P.	Barrister & Baronet	1872	UNSIGNED
Gordon, The Rt. Hon. E. Strathearn	Lord Advocate	1874	APE
Grantham, Sir William	Mr. Justice Grantham	1890	SPY
Grimthorpe, The Rt. Hon. Lord	Bells	1889	SPY
Group	Bench and Bar	1891	STUFF
Group	Heads of the Law	1902	SPY

SUBJECT	CAPTION	YEAR	ARTIST
Group	Purse, Pussy, Piety	1882	T
Grove, The Hon. Sir William Robert	Galvanic Electricity	1887	SPY

H

SUBJECT	CAPTION	YEAR	ARTIST
Haldane, Mr. R. Burdon, Q.C., M.P.	A Hegelian Politician	1896	SPY
Haldane, Lord	A Government Marked	1913	OWL
Hall, Mr. Charles, Q.C., M.P.	Charley	1888	SPY
Halsbury, Lord	From The Old Bailey	1890	SPY
Hannen, The Rt. Hon. Sir James, KT., P.C.	The Great Unmarrier	1888	SPY
Hastie, Mr. A.H.	He Is A Smart Fellow	1893	SPY
Hatherley, Lord	When He Who Has	1869	APE
Hatherton, Lord	Lord Hatherton	1895	STUFF-G
Hawkins, Mr. Henry, Q.C.	The Tichborne Case	1873	SPY
Healy, Mr. Timothy Michael, M.P.	Tim	1886	SPY
Helder, Mr. August, M.P.	Whitehaven	1896	SPY
Hemmerde, Mr. Edward G., K.C.	The New Recorder	1909	SPY
Hemphill, Mr. Charles Hare, K.C., M.P.	The Irish Serjeant	1904	SPY
Herschell, Sir Farrer, M.P., Q.C.	The Solicitor General	1881	SPY
Holker, Sir John	Attorney General	1878	SPY
Holmes, Dr. Oliver Wendell	The Autocrat of the Breakfast Table	1886	SPY
Howard, Mr. Morgan, Q.C.	Energetic Toryism	1881	SPY
Huddleston, Mr. John W., Q.C., M.P.	A Future Judge	1874	APE
Huntington, Sir C.P.	Tubby	1910	QUIP
Hutchinson, Mr. C.C., K.C.	Hutchy	1911	APE JR

I

SUBJECT	CAPTION	YEAR	ARTIST
Inderwick, Mr. Frederick Andrew, Q.C.	Divorce Court	1896	SPY
Isaacs, Mr. Rufus Daniel, K.C., M.P.	Rufus	1904	SPY

J

SUBJECT	CAPTION	YEAR	ARTIST
James, Sir Henry, M.P.	Nervous	1874	APE
Jelf, Mr. Arthur Richard, Q.C.	Oxford Circuit	1896	SPY
Jelf, The Hon. Sir Arthur Richard, K.C.	Ermined Urbanity	1904	SPY
Jessel, The Rt. Hon. Sir George	The Law	1879	SPY
Jeune, The Hon. Sir Francis Henry	Matrimonial Causes	1891	STUFF
Jones, Mr. Atherley, K.C., M.P.	Jonesy	1912	WH
Joyce, The Hon. Sir Matthew Ingle	Steady-Going	1902	SPY

K

SUBJECT	CAPTION	YEAR	ARTIST
Kay, The Hon. Sir Edward Ebenezer	Costs Disallowed	1888	SPY
Kekewich, The Hon. Sir Arthur	A Hasty Judge	1895	SPY
Kelly, The Rt. Hon. Sir Fitz Roy Edward	The Lord Chief Baron	1871	COIDE
Kenealy, Dr. Edward Vaughan	The Claimant's Counsel	1873	SPY
Kennedy, The Hon. Sir W.R.	Our Weakest Judge	1893	SPY
Kerr, Mr. Commissioner	The City of London Court	1900	SPY

L

SUBJECT	CAPTION	YEAR	ARTIST
Lawrance, Mr. Justice	Long Lawrance	1897	SPY
Lawrence, Mr. Justice A.T.	Lorry	1907	SPY
Leeman, Mr. George, M.P.	A Yorkshire Solicitor	1872	UNSIGNED
Lefevre, Sir John George Shaw, K.C.B.	La Reyne Le Veult	1871	APE
Lewis, Mr. George Henry	An Astute Lawyer	1876	SPY
Liddell, The Hon. Sir Adolphus Frederick Octavius, K.C.B., Q.C.	Dodo	1882	SPY
Lindley, Sir Nathaniel	Partnership	1890	SPY
Lockwood, Mr. Frank, Q.C., M.P.	York	1887	SPY
Lopes, The Rt. Hon. Sir H.C.	An Old-Fashioned Judge	1893	QUIZ
Lush, Mr. Justice	Like Father, Like Son	1911	APE JR
Lush, The Hon. Sir Robert	A Little Lush	1873	SPY
Lushington, Mr. Franklin	He Believe in the Police	1899	SPY

SUBJECT	CAPTION	YEAR	ARTIST

M

SUBJECT	CAPTION	YEAR	ARTIST
McCall, Mr. Robert Alfred, K.C.	Ulsterman K.C.	1903	SPY
MacDonald, The Rt. Hon. Col. John		1875	APE
Hay Athole, C.B., Q.C., M.P., J.P., D.L.	The Lord Advocate	1888	SPY
MacNeill, Mr. John Gordon Swift, K.C.	South Donegal	1902	SPY
MacNaghten, Baron, P.C.	He Succeeded Lord Blackburn	1895	SPY
Manisty, Mr. Justice	Mr. Justice Manisty	1889	QUIZ
Marriott, Mr. William Thackeray, M.P., Q.C.	Brighton	1883	T
Mathew, Mr. Justice	Commercial Court	1896	SPY
Mathews, Mr. Charles Willie	He Can Marshall Evidence	1892	SPY
Matthews, The Rt. Hon. Henry, Q.C., M.P.	The Home Secretary	1887	SPY
May, Sir Thomas Erskine, K.C.B.	Parliamentary Practice	1871	APE
Mellish, The Rt. Hon. Sir George D.C.L.	Appeals	1876	SPY
Mellor, The Hon. Sir John	Judges the Claimant	1873	SPY
Morgan, Mr. George Osborne, Q.C., M.P.	Burials	1879	SPY
Morris of Spiddal, Lord	An Irish Lawyer	1893	SPY
Moulton, Mr. John Fletcher	Patents	1900	SPY
Murphy, Mr. John Patrick	For The Times	1889	SPY
Murray, The Rt. Hon. Andrew	Lord Advocate	1896	SPY

N

SUBJECT	CAPTION	YEAR	ARTIST
Newton, Mr. A.J.E.	The Marlborough Street Solicitor	1893	SPY
North, The Hon. Sir Ford	Gentle Manners	1887	SPY

O

SUBJECT	CAPTION	YEAR	ARTIST
Onslow, Mr. Guildford James Hillier Mainwaring Ellerker	The Claimant's Friend	1875	APE

P

SUBJECT	CAPTION	YEAR	ARTIST
Palmer, Mr. John Hinde, Q.C., M.P.	Lincoln	1883	SPY
Parry, Sergeant	A Lawyer	1873	SPY
Peel, The Rt. Hon. Arthur Wellesley, P.C., M.P.	The Speaker	1887	SPY
Penzance, Lord	A Judge & Peer	1869	UNK
Phillimore, The Hon. Sir Walter George Frank, Bart., D.C.L.	A Judicial Churchman	1898	SPY
Pitt-Lewis, Mr. George, Q.C., M.P.	Barnstaple	1887	SPY
Poland, Mr. Henry Bodkin	For the Crown	1886	SPY
Pollock, Sir Charles Edward	One Of The Family	1890	QUIZ
Pollock, The Rt. Hon. Sir Frederick	A Souvenir	1870	ATN
Pope, Mr. Samuel, Q.C.	Jumbo	1885	SPY
Pridham-Wippel, Mr. P.H.	Pridham	1910	ELF

R

SUBJECT	CAPTION	YEAR	ARTIST
Rawle, Mr. Thomas	The President of the Law	1905	SPY
Rawlinson, Mr. J.F.P., K.C., M.P.	Eton and Cambridge	1908	SPY
Reid, Sir Robert Threshie, Q.C., M.P.	Mr. Attorney	1895	SPY
Ridley, Mr. Justice	The New Judge	1897	FTD
Rigby, Lord Justice	A Blunt Lord Justice	1901	SPY
Rigby, Sir J., Q.C.	Mr. Solicitor	1893	STUFF
Robson, Sir W.S., K.C., M.P.	The Solicitor General	1906	SPY
Rollit, Sir Albert Kaye, K.T., LL.D., M.P.	Municipal Corporations	1886	SPY
Romer, The Hon. Sir Robert	Bob	1891	STUFF
Rose, Sir Philip, Bart.	Lord Beaconsfield's Friend	1881	SPY
Russell, Mr. Charles, Q.C., M.P.	A Splendid Advocate	1883	UNSIGNED
Russell, The Hon. Mr. Charles	A Son of His Father	1907	SPY
Russell, Sir Charles, Q.C.	Cross Examination	1890	QUIZ
Russell, Sir George	Wokingham	1889	SPY

S

SUBJECT	CAPTION	YEAR	ARTIST
Scrutton, Mr. Justice	Copyright	1911	APE JR
Shand, The Baron	A Scots Lawyer	1903	SPY
Simon, Sir John, K.C.	Simple Simon	1911	WH
Simon, Sir John, K.T., M.P. Serjeant-at-law	The Serjeant	1886	SPY

SUBJECT	CAPTION	YEAR	ARTIST
Smith, The Hon. Sir Archibald Levin	3rd Commissioner	1888	SPY
Smith, Mr. F.E., M.P.	A Successful First Speech	1907	SPY
Smith, Mr. F.E., K.C., M.P.	No Surrender	1911	NIBS
Stephen, Sir James F.	The Criminal Code	1885	SPY
Stirling, Mr. Justice	Equity	1897	SPY
Straight, The Hon. Mr. Justice	The New Judge	1879	SPY

T

Thring, Lord	He Has Written	1893	SPY

V

Vaughan, James	Bow Street	1890	SPY

W

Walton, Mr. John Lawson, K.C.	A Radical Lawyer	1902	SPY
Walton, The Hon. Sir Joseph	A Lawyer on the Bench	1902	SPY
Warmington, Mr. Cornelius Marshall	Directors' Liability	1891	STUFF
Warrington, Hon. Mr. Justice Rolls	A Very Sound Judge	1907	SPY
Webster, Mr. Richard Everard, Q.C.	Law and Conscience	1883	UNSIGNED
Williams, Sir Roland Vaughan	The Mandarin	1890	QUIZ
Williams, Lord Justice	A Rustic Judge	1899	CGD
Wills, Mr. Justice	Benevolence On The Bench	1896	SPY
Witt, Sir John George, Q.C.	A Sporting Lawyer	1898	SPY
Wright, Mr. Justice	He Declined Knighthood	1891	STUFF

Appendix B

Admiralty Jurisdiction	Barnes	1893		Eton & Cambridge	Rawlinson	1908
An Amiable Judge	Channell	1898		Exchequer, The	Bramwell	1876
An Arbitrator	Bramwell	1892				
An Astute Lawyer	Lewis	1876		Fair if not Beautiful	Cozens-Hardy	1901
Appeals	Mellish	1876		First of the Commoners, The	Denison	1870
As Procureur General	Beaurepaire	1893		Formerly of the Carlton	Cleasby	1876
Attorney General	Holker	1878		For The Crown	Poland	1886
Australia	Barton	1902		For The Times	Murphy	1889
Autocrat of the Breakfast				From the Old Bailey	Halsbury	1890
Table, The	Holmes	1886		Future Judge, A	Huddleston	1874
Bargrave	Deane	1898		Galvanic Electricity	Grove	1887
Barnstaple	Pitt-Lewis	1887		Gentle Manners	North	1887
Barrister & Baronet	Goldsmid	1872		George	Elliott	1908
Bells	Grimthorpe	1889		Gill Brass	Gill	1891
Bench & Bar	Group	1891		Good Form	Bankes	1906
Benevolence On The Bench	Wills	1896		Good Judge A	Eve	1911
Billy	Belilios	1910		Government Married	Haldane	1913
Birth, Behaviour & Business	Bright	1881		Great Orator, A	Asquith	1910
Blunt Lord Justice, A	Rigby	1901		Great Unmarrier, The	Hannen	1888
Bob	Romer	1891		Guileless	Cotton	1888
Bosey, Frederick	Bosanquet	1901				
Bow Street	Vaughan	1890		Hard Head	Finlay	1888
Brains	Asquith	1904		Hasty Judge, A	Kekewich	1895
Brighton	Marriott	1883		Heads of Law	Group	1902
Burials	Morgan	1879		He believes in the Police	Lushington	1899
				He can Marshall Evidence	Mathews	1892
Charley	Hall	1888		He Declined Knighthood	Wright	1891
Chitty's Leader	Byrne	1896		He Defended Arabi	Broadley	1889
City Justice	Carden	1880		He has Leathern Lungs	Cock	1891
City of London Court, The	Kerr	1900		He Has Written	Thring	1893
Claimant's Counsel, The	Kenealy	1873		He Is A Smart Fellow	Hastie	1893
Claimant's Friend, The	Onslow	1875		He Resisted Temptation	Ballantine	1870
Commercial Court	Mathew	1896		He Succeeded Lord Blackburn	MacNaghten	1895
Company Law	Buckley	1900		He Was An Ornament	Denman	1892
Conciliator, The	Askwith	1911		Hegelian Politician, A	Haldane	1896
Contempt of Court	Bacon	1873		His Father Invented Pickwick	Dickens	1897
Copyright	Scrutton	1911		Holborn	Bruce	1892
Costs Disallowed	Kay	1888		Home Secretary, The	Matthews	1887
Court of Appeals, The	Baggallay	1875		Hutchy	Hutchinson	1911
Court Roll	Elton	1887				
Criminal Code, The	Stephen	1885		I Never Ask Anyone	Carson	1912
Cross Examination	Russell	1890		Irish Lawyer, An	Morris	1893
				Irish Serjeant, The	Hemphill	1904
Danky	Danckwerts	1898		Irish Wit, An	Dowse	1871
Deceased Wife's Sister, The	Chambers	1884				
Dick	Alverstone	1900		Jonesy	Jones	1912
Directors' Liability	Warmington	1891		Judge & Peer, A	Penzance	1869
Divorce	Bitt	1887		Judges The Claimant	Mellor	1873
Divorce Court	Inderwick	1896		Judicial Churchman, A	Phillimore	1898
Dodo	Liddell	1882		Judicial Joker, A	Bacon	1897
Dublin University	Carson	1893		Judicial Lightweight	Darling	1907
Dublin University	Carson	1911		Judicial Politeness	Bowen	1892
Dublin University	Gibson	1885		Jumbo	Pope	1885
				Justice to Dreyfus	Brisson	1898
East Fife	Asquith	1891				
Energetic Toryism	Howard	1892		Knight of Malta, The	Bowyer	1879
Ermined Urbanity	Jelf	1904				
Equity	Stirling	1897				

La Reyne Le Veult	Lefèvre	1871
Law	Ellenborough	1886
Law, The	Jessell	1879
Law and Conscience	Webster	1883
Lawyer on the Bench, The	Walton	1902
Lawyer, A	Parry	1873
Like Father Like Son	Lush	1911
Lincoln	Palmer	1883
Little Darling	Darling	1897
Little Lush, A	Lush	1873
London Sessions	Edlin	1891
Long Lawrance	Lawrance	1897
Lord Advocate, The	Balfour	1886
Lord Advocate	Gordon	1874
Lord Advocate, The	MacDonald	1888
Lord Advocate	Murray	1896
Lord Beaconsfield's Friend	Rose	1881
Lord Chief Baron, The	Kelly	1871
Lord Chief Justice	Alverstone	1913
Lord Chief Justice, The	Cockburn	1869
Lord Chief Justice, The	Coleridge	1887
Lord Hatherton	Hatherton	1895
Lord Justice Barry	Barry	1889
Lord of Appeal, A	Blackburn	1881
Lorry	Lawrence	1907
Majesty of the law, The	Bovill	1870
Mandarin, The	Williams	1890
Man of Law and Broad Acres, A	Bray	1906
Marlborough Street Solicitor, The	Newton	1893
Matrimonial Causes	Jeune	1891
Mid Armagh	Barton	1898
Mr. Attorney	Reid	1895
Mr. Justice Grantham	Grantham	1890
Mr. Justice Manisty	Manisty	1889
Mr. Solicitor	Rigby	1893
Municipal Corporations	Rollit	1886
Nervous	James	1874
New Judge, The	Charles	1888
New Judge, The	Ridley	1897
New Judge, The	Straight	1879
New Recorder, The	Hemmerde	1909
Northeast Bethnal Green	Bhownaggree	1897
North London	Fordham	1908
North Norfolk	Cozens-Hardy	1893
No Surrender	Smith F.E.	1911
Old-Fashioned Judge, An	Lopes	1893
One of the Family	Pollock	1890
Our Weakest Judge	Kennedy	1893
Oxford Circuit	Jelf	1896
Parliamentary practice	May	1871
Partnership	Lindley	1890
Patents	Moulton	1900
Plausible	Eady	1902
Popular Judgement	Brett	1876
Popular Magistrate, A	Baggallay	1905
Powers	Farwell	1900
President of the Law, The	Rawle	1905
Pridham	Pridham-Wippel	1910
Public Prosecutions	Desart	1902
Purse, Pussy, Piety	Group	1882
Radical Lawyer, A	Walton	1902
Recorder, The	Fulton	1903
Risen Barrister, A	Coleridge	1870
Rufus	Isaacs	1904
Rustic Judge A	Williams	1899
Scotch Law	Colonsay	1873
Scots Lawyer, A	Shand	1903
2nd Commissioner	Day	1888
Serjeant, The	Simon	1886
Silvered Voice, The	Coleridge	1909
Simple Simon	Simon	1911
Sir Edward	Clarke	1903
Sir John Coleridge	Collier	1870
Slim	Avory	1904
Slow and Steady	Bruce	1900
Smith's Leading Cases	Collins	1893
Solicitor General, The	Buckmastter	1913
Solicitor General, The	Giffard	1878
Solicitor General, The	Herschell	1881
Solicitor General, The	Robson	1906
Son of His Father, A	Russell	1907
South Bucks	Curzon	1896
South Donegal	MacNeill	1902
Souvenir, A	Pollock	1870
So Voluble an Advocate	Cecil	1906
Speaker, The	Peel	1887
Specific Performance	Fry	1891
Splendid Advocate, A	Russell	1883
Sporting Lawyer, A	Witt	1898
Stay Please	Field	1887
Steady-Going	Joyce	1902
Successful First Speech, A	Smith F., E.	1907
3rd Commissioner	Smith A.L.	1888
Tichborne Case, The	Hawkins	1873
Tim	Healy	1886
That Won't Do, You Know	Cave	1893
Tommy	Bucknill	1900
Tubby	Huntington	1910
Ulsterman KC	McCall	1903
Umpire, The	Chitty	1885
Under Sheriff	Beard	1891
Very Sound Judge, A	Warrington	1907
Vicar General	Cripps	1902
We Shall See	Bigham	1898
When He Who Has	Hatherley	1869
Whitehaven	Helder	1896
Wokingham	Russell	1889
Worship Street	Biron	1907
York	Lockwood	1887
York City	Butcher	1901
Yorkshire Solicitor, A	Leeman	1872